Becoming an Emotionally Healthy School

Becoming an Emotionally Healthy School

Auditing and developing the National Healthy
School Standard for 5 to 11 year olds

Charlie Smith
Shall McKee

P·C·P
Paul Chapman
Publishing

Paul Chapman Publishing
A SAGE Publications Company
1 Oliver's Yard
55 City Road
London EC1Y 1SP

SAGE Publications Inc.
2455 Teller Road
Thousand Oaks, California 91320

SAGE Publications India Pvt Ltd
B-42, Panchsheel Enclave
Post Box 4109
New Delhi 110 017

Commissioning Editor: George Robinson
Editorial Team: Mel Maines, Sarah Lynch, Wendy Ogden, Mike Gibbs
Designer: Helen Weller

A catalogue record for this book is available from the British Library

Library of Congress Control Number: 2005929001

ISBN 1-4129-1187-7

Printed on paper from sustainable resources.

Printed in Great Britain by The Cromwell Press Ltd, Trowbridge, Wiltshire

Contents

Preface   vii

Chapter One: Introduction   1

The National Healthy Schools Standard   1
The Benefits of Being Involved in the National Healthy
    Schools Standard   2
Ten Areas of Whole-school Improvement   4
Themes from the Healthy School Standard   4
Links with Emotional Health and Wellbeing   16
The Emotional Health and Wellbeing Theme of
    the National Schools Standard   25

**Chapter Two: Developing the Emotional Health
and Wellbeing (Including Bullying) Standard**   27

The Process   27
Step One: Make a Decision on the Theme   28
Step Two: Allocate a Co-ordinator and Develop a Task Group   29
Step Three: Needs Analysis – An Emotional Health and
    Wellbeing Audit   33
Step Four: Feed Back Findings   47
Step Five: Develop an Action Plan   47
Step Six: Implementing the Plan   50
Step Seven: Submitting the Evidence   51
Step Eight: Receiving Accreditation   52
Step Nine: Celebrate   53
Step Ten: Ongoing Reviews   53
Healthy Schools Action Plan: An Example   55

**Chapter Three: Preparing for an Emotional Health
and Wellbeing Programme**   61

Programme Content   61
Programme Application   65
Setting up an Emotional Health and Wellbeing
    Programme with Small and One-off Groups   66
Using the Programme to Gain the National Healthy
    Schools Standard   79

Chapter Four: Emotional Health and Wellbeing
Sessions for Key Stage 1 Pupils   81

Session 1: This is Me   83
Session 2: Feelings   86
Session 3: Communication   89
Session 4: Choices   93
Session 5: Personal Safety   98
Session 6: Keeping Others Safe   106
Session 7: Relationships   111
Session 8: Difference   115

Chapter Five: Emotional Health and Wellbeing
Sessions for Key Stage 2 Pupils   119

Session 1: This is Me   121
Session 2: Feelings   126
Session 3: Communication   129
Session 4: Choices   131
Session 5: Personal Safety   133
Session 6: Keeping Others Safe   136
Session 7: Relationships   138
Session 8: Difference   141

Bibliography and Resources   147

The CD-ROM contains PDF files, labelled 'Worksheets.pdf' which consists of worksheets for each lesson in this resource. You will need Acrobat Reader version 3 or higher to view and print these resources.

The documents are set up to print to A4 but you can enlarge them to A3 by increasing the output percentage at the point of printing using the page set-up settings for your printer.

To photocopy the worksheets directly from this book, set your photocopier to enlarge by 125% and align the edge of the page to be copied against the leading edge of the copier glass (usually indicated by an arrow).

Preface

The aims of this book are to help your school achieve the National Healthy School Standard through the theme of Emotional Health and Wellbeing Including Bullying. The book will provide the reader with:

- an overview of the National Healthy School Standard (NHSS)

- insight into the theme of emotional health

- a range of case-studies to draw on as exemplars of good practice in developing the theme of emotional health and wellbeing

- knowledge and resources required to undertake a school based audit on emotional health and wellbeing (including bullying)

- resources to carry out a programme that could be run with pupils to implement the standard throughout school while at the same time meet the requirements for PSHE and Citizenship.

The purpose of this book is to help school staff, people working with schools and healthy schools co-ordinators create, develop and promote a whole-school approach to emotional health and wellbeing (including bullying).

If the school is working towards the NHSS through the theme of emotional health it is advised that the school follow the process that this book offers:

- develop a task group

- undertake a needs analysis/audit

- set whole-school targets

- agree a plan of action

- implement the curriculum alongside any other ventures the school is intending to do

- review the action.

This book offers advice, handy hints and support at each stage of the process and provides all the resources that will be required. It is advised that the school liaises with their local healthy schools co-ordinator and incorporates any regionally defined practices (for example, the school may find that their Local Education Authority has a specific audit tool).

Chapter One

Introduction

The term 'development' refers to the process of growth and change; as humans we develop constantly from conception into infancy through adolescence and into adulthood. Throughout our lifespan we develop in a range of ways – socially, emotionally and intellectually. According to Maslow (1954) we are subject to two quite different sets of motivational states or forces. Firstly those which ensure survival by satisfying basic physical and psychological needs (physiological, safety, belonging, love and esteem needs), and secondly those which promote the person's self-actualisation, that is, realising one's full potential – 'becoming capable of everything that one is capable of becoming' (Maslow 1970). In relation to healthy child development Carl Rogers (1961) believed that whether these needs are fulfilled depends on how far the adults around young people (at home, at school and in the community) can look after them and create the right conditions for them to grow emotionally, socially and intellectually. All young people deserve the awareness, support and efforts of the adults around them to develop into fully rounded human beings with the strength and capacity to live a full and creative life (Danson et al, 1997) and educators are in a prime position to help, support and guide young people in their social, social and intellectual development.

The National Healthy Schools Standard

It is evident that pupils can fulfil their potential only when they are healthy, happy and at ease in all areas of their lives and the National Healthy Schools Standard (NHSS) is designed to give practical support for school to create this environment – an enjoyable, safe, productive learning environment that minimises potential health risks (DfEE, 1999). The NHSS is an accreditation process for education and health partnerships. The initiative was launched by the Department of Health and Education and Employment in 1999, with the aims of reducing health inequalities, promoting social inclusion and raising educational achievement. Each authority has a 'Healthy Schools' programme that will help schools through the process of the accreditation, and monitor and assess the schools standards in becoming and sustaining a healthy school.

The term 'health' holds many connotations: when we think about health we may consider mental health, physical wellbeing, emotional ability or personal development. So what does it mean to be a healthy school? The Department for Education and Employment (DfEE) in the National Healthy School Standard Guidance outline that a healthy school is:

> ... one that is successful in helping pupils to do their best and build on their achievements. It is committed to ongoing improvement and development. It promotes physical and emotional health by providing accessible and relevant information and equipping pupils with the skills and attitudes to make informed decisions about their health. A healthy school understands the importance in investing in health to assist in the process of raising levels of pupil achievement and improving standards. It also recognises the need to provide both a physical and social environment that is conducive to learning.

> (DfEE, 1999b, p2).

This is not something new for schools but a way of enhancing good practice holistically and throughout school life. The accreditation will help establish consistent and rigorous standards across partnerships and schools and help ensure we are providing the most conducive learning environments for our children and young people in schools.

The Benefits of Being Involved in the National Healthy Schools Standard

A healthy school by terms of the definition above will have an enormous positive impact on both the staff and pupils alike.

The DfEE (1999a) state that 'as well as having happier, healthier pupils and better motivated staff, signing up to the NHSS will lift your school performance and add value in a number of ways.' They go on to list the influences on pupils, schools and communities; these include the following:

Pupils

- more confident
- more motivated
- better life and health choices
- higher academic achievement
- improved access to support services
- valued personal and social development
- more able to reach individual potential.

Schools

- improved academic and non-academic performance
- improved community and parental links
- whole-school involvement
- stronger external partnerships
- improved staff development
- greater coherence between initiatives
- positive school promotion
- improved reputation and status.

Communities

- reduction in truancy, crime, teenage pregnancy and drug use
- improved citizenship
- closer ties between school, health authorities, social services, police and other agencies
- greater community contribution to school life.

A report by the National Health Service (NHS 2002) says that the evidence gathered by a large number of agencies – including Ofsted, Glasgow University, a national audit and independent evaluations of local programmes – clearly shows that the structure and process of the NHSS are making a difference in terms of education and health improvement. The key findings show that schools engaging with the NHSS are more likely to be improving their standards at a faster rate than the national average, and the NHSS is having a greater influence in schools serving areas of socio-economic disadvantage.

Ten Areas of Whole-school Improvement

In order for a school to achieve the NHSS they need to ensure a holistic approach is adopted and that they embrace a whole-school approach to change, development and support.

> Picking up a few aspects of the Healthy School Standard and introducing it in a piecemeal way won't work. Likewise, if it is driven only by a small group without involvement from the wider school community, it won't be effective.

> (DfEE, 1999a)

To show that the school engages everyone – parents/carers, pupils, staff, governors and partner agencies – in the process they need to show school activity in ten areas:

1. Leadership, management and managing change

2. Policy development

3. Curriculum planning, resourcing and working with external agencies

4. Teaching and learning

5. School culture and environment

6. Giving pupils a voice

7. Provision of pupils' support services

8. Staff professional development needs, health and welfare

9. Partnerships with parents, carers and local communities

10. Assessing, recording and reporting pupils' achievements.

Once the school has chosen a specific theme or set of themes to work on, as outlined below, they will need to ensure that the theme is then implemented in all of these ten areas. The benefits of this are instrumental to the success of becoming a healthy school.

Themes from the Healthy School Standard

Within the NHSS there are eight themes around education and health that schools can address:

1. Personal, Social and Health Education

2. Citizenship

3. Drug Education

4. Emotional Health and Wellbeing (including bullying)

5. Healthy Eating

6. Physical Activity

7. Personal Safety

8. Sex and Relationship Education.

Personal Social and Health Education

Personal, Social and Health Education (PSHE) is a fairly recent addition to the curriculum in England; it is a curriculum that enables a pupil to clarify their own values. PSHE is about learning how to cope with the different things that you may encounter as you grow up, and in your later life. Personal education is concerned with the emotional health and wellbeing of the individual. Social education is intended to develop collectivism and group thinking. Health education covers eating, healthy lifestyle and drug, sex and relationship education.

National Healthy School Standard, DfEE, 1999b

- The school recognises that all aspects of school life have an impact on the personal and social development of pupils and that consistent messages are presented.

- The school encourages pupils to recognise their achievements and do their best.

Case-study

Schools have taken PSHE forward in a wide range of creative ways. One way this has been achieved is through the allocation of a PSHE co-ordinator, someone who is responsible for designing 'fun' resources and ensuring all teachers are able to implement PSHE themes with their classes. The PSHE co-ordinator can help other staff deliver Circle Time based sessions with pupils to deliver themes in the PSHE curriculum. Having allocated time for PSHE, rather than it being a bolt on activity, has proved useful in many schools in enhancing the social, emotional and behavioural development of its pupils. Many primary schools have used the dynamics of Circle Time to run PSHE, i.e. remove tables, sit pupils in a circle, use a range of facilitation techniques and ensure that an ethos of safety is created to discuss the topics.

Citizenship

The National Curriculum in England has included Citizenship since September 2002. There is a framework for primary schools and a statutory requirement for secondary schools. Citizenship gives pupils the knowledge, skills and understanding to play an effective role in society. Citizenship education has three strands:

1. Social and moral responsibility: pupils learn, from the beginning, self-confidence and socially and morally responsible behaviour.

2. Community involvement: pupils learn how to become helpfully involved in the life and concerns of their neighbourhood and communities.

3. Political literacy: pupils learn about the institutions, issues, problems and practices of our democracy and how citizens can make themselves effective in public life. (DfES, 2002)

National Healthy School Standard, DfEE, 1999b

- The school recognises that all aspects of school life can have an impact on the development of pupils in becoming informed, active and responsible citizens.

- The school provides opportunities for pupils to be actively involved in the life of their school and communities.

Case-study

One method schools have applied to make citizenship 'real' is to ensure that the actual activities are focused within and impact upon the local community. For example, when looking at the theme of community involvement one school decided to work with pupils to build bird feeding tables and approach local businesses to supply or provide funding for bird seed. The pupils designed and made the bird tables and were then responsible, working with the local council, for setting up the bird tables in local parks and gardens; volunteers from the community were sought to help maintain the tables and ensure new food was put out. The pupils also wrote up projects, made contributions to other subject areas such as maths and art and design and wrote up about the effects of their efforts on the environment and local community. The theme of community involvement was addressed while at the same time the pupils were engaged in a project in which they made a real difference short and long-term as a citizen and community member.

Drug Education (including alcohol and tobacco)

A school's response to, and education about, drugs can cover various issues:

- drug usage

- applying intervention for a drugs related issue

- prevention and awareness raising work

- peer pressure

- first-aid

- drug law

- effects and risks.

Some schools have peer education programmes, others appoint mentors and many schools now build in drugs education to their PSHE curriculum. There are many ways that schools now deliver drugs awareness and drugs education programmes to young people, however, even the most proactive schools with advanced programmes of intervention can't eradicate drugs, alcohol and tobacco from the pupils' wider social community and environment.

National Healthy School Standard, DfEE, 1999b

- The school has a named member of staff and a governor who are responsible for drug education provision.

- The school has a planned drug education programme involving development of skills, starting from early years, which identifies learning outcomes, appropriate to pupils' age, ability and level of maturity and which is based on pupils' needs assessment.

- The school has a policy, owned and implemented by the whole school, including parents/carers, for managing drug related incidents which includes identifying sources of support for pupils and alternatives to exclusion.

- Staff understand the role that schools can play in the national drug strategy and are confident to discuss drugs issues and services with pupils.

- The school works with the police, youth service and local drug services in line with the Drug Action Team strategy to develop its understanding of local issues and to inform its policy.

One school used Persona Dolls (cloth dolls) to deliver substance safety education to children aged four to seven. Drugs were explored by using the key message that the 'behaviour is a choice' and by using a technique called 'one step removed'. One step removed is about children talking about their experiences and ideas through characters. The technique surmises that sometimes children can be inhibited about sharing their ideas or experiences with their peers due to the risk of being judged or excluded, therefore if we create a forum whereby children are talking about characters and not themselves this removes the onus of what they are saying being about them, while at the same time allowing children to openly express their ideas and experiences. Children can and will only talk about what they know. With drugs education this approach has been used by introducing the dolls into a classroom and enabling pupils to discover each doll's persona. The dolls become part of the class and when discussing each doll's persona, thoughts and feelings the pupils can express their own thoughts and feelings around these issues, which are often difficult and challenging to explore.

Emotional Health and Wellbeing (including Bullying)

Emotional health and wellbeing

Emotional Health and Wellbeing underpins all of the key themes; it is about an individual's capacity to recognise, understand and effectively manage and express feelings and show concern for the feelings of others in a mutually supportive environment (White et al, 2002). It is also about self-esteem, self-identity, self-worth and self-respect and about an individual having the ability to make informed decisions about their lives. How we feel about ourselves, others and our environment plays a vital role in creating and maintaining healthy relationships and influences the strength of those relationships. How we feel about ourselves and others is also directly related to the values and attitudes contained within our social groups, the ability to respond and make safe choices and the self-confidence we have to learn and grow and care for ourselves and others. How we feel about ourselves, others and the world around us, affects the way we respond and cope to all that life has to throw at us. Therefore it is essential that time is spent allowing the whole school community to build a deep and positive sense of wellbeing and a strong emotional self to help us face life's challenges with confidence, whilst remaining within a nurturing environment that respects everyone's right to feel safe.

Bullying

Bullying behaviour can have a profound effect on the way in which pupils feel about themselves (self-esteem) and on their education. Bullying in schools is no doubt a very old phenomenon but it was not until fairly recently that efforts were made to systematically study it. A strong societal interest in bullying in schools began when in a northern part of Norway in 1982, a newspaper reported that three 10-14 year old boys had committed suicide; in all probability as a consequence of severe bullying by peers. In England we only have to look to our own newspapers to see continued reports of bullying, including verbal abuse, physical abuse and emotional abuse – one national story was about text message bullying among girls, a case so severe that it ended up in court. Following such horrific reports a national campaign aimed at the systematic reduction of bullying was launched in numerous counties.

Bullying can be described as behaviour that causes or intends to cause physical, emotional or verbal harm to another; examples of such behaviour include name-calling, shunning, hitting and spreading rumours. Bullying is usually considered as such when it takes place on more than one occasion over a prolonged period of time.

> The emotional distress caused by bullying in whatever form, be it racial, or as a result of a child's appearance, behaviour or special educational needs, or related to sexual orientation, can prejudice school achievement, lead to lateness or truancy, and in extreme cases, end in suicide... Low rates should not themselves be taken as proof bullying is not occurring. (Dept for Education & Employment, 1999)

Evidence suggests that consideration for the physical and emotional wellbeing of pupils and implementing preventative work around bullying behaviour can create a safer school environment as well as raise academic achievement. For this to be accomplished the whole school needs to be proactive in creating and sustaining a safer environment for all.

National Healthy School Standard, DfEE, 1999b

- Opportunities are provided for pupils' views to inform policy and practice.
- The school has a policy and code of practice for tackling bullying, which is owned, understood and implemented by all members of

the school community and includes contact with external support agencies.

- The school openly addresses issues of emotional health and wellbeing by enabling pupils to understand what they are feeling and by building their confidence to learn.

- The school identifies and supports the emotional health needs of staff.

Case-study 1: Emotional Health

A feelings tree was erected in the foyer of one primary school reception area. A potted tree was donated to the school; parents/carers, pupils, teachers and community visitors to the school were encouraged to attach objects to the tree including pictures and photographs, with thought and feeling words printed on the reverse. This proved to be a great success with the school and demonstrated the ethos and culture of the school, that is, that everyone's thoughts, feelings, dreams and aspirations were known and accepted by all.

The school decided to take this concept one step further to help identify pupils' feelings in the classroom and thus helping teachers to be more aware of the emotional climate of their classroom. Each classroom had an 'Ocean of Emotion' display by the door. The display consisted of a picture of the sea with lots of fish on it that were detachable by using Velcro, on each fish was a feeling word. As children came into the classroom at the start of the day they were asked to choose a fish from the Ocean of Emotion that described how they were feeling at that particular moment. The pupils simply put the fish next to them on their desk. By doing this the teacher had insight into the range of feeling pupils were experiencing and if necessary used the classroom assistant to help talk through any emotions that children had that may have been a block to their learning, prior to them engaging in the lesson. Pupils were also encouraged throughout the course of the lesson to change the emotion should their feeling radically change; again this helped give teachers insight into how different activities led pupils to feel, and address this accordingly. As a means of a role model the teacher also picked a fish and could change their fish throughout the lesson accordingly. The reason the school adopted this technique was that if children were in a climate emotionally conducive to learning then they would learn more and, in reverse, that if emotionally children were not ready for learning to take place then their recall of the lesson content would be poor.

Many schools are now using Peer Educators to help address bullying behaviour in school. One school decided to train a small group of pupils in listening and supporting skills. They then put on a drama performance in assembly to introduce the concept of bullying and its effects. After the performance half a day was allocated to running follow-up workshops around bullying. External agencies and the Peer Educators were involved in the workshop delivery. Pupils were encouraged to take any further questions they had, or support they wanted on bullying issues to the Peer Educators, who set up a drop-in service for pupils to access at lunch-times.

Healthy Eating

The latest National Nutritional Standards for school lunches (a compulsory requirement for LEA caterers as of April 2001) can provide a starting point for schools to look at the theme of 'healthy eating'. Attitudes about what constitutes healthy eating vary considerably due to the multitude of influences from the media and while we may all think we know what healthy eating is it is evident that children and adults consume too many foods high in saturated fats, salt and sugar and lack the foods rich in vitamins and minerals.

What's important is to ensure that any programme around healthy eating contributes to whole-school improvement and provides a commitment to a whole-school approach to healthy eating and the development of positive attitudes towards food. This could range from schools providing access to fresh, clean drinking water for pupils and staff to enabling pupils to make informed choices on healthy eating that will allow them to fulfil their potential.

National Healthy School Standard, DfEE, 1999b

- The school presents consistent, informed messages about healthy eating, for example, food on offer in vending machines, tuck shops and school meals should complement the taught curriculum.

- The school provides, promotes and monitors healthier food at lunch and breaktimes and in any breakfast clubs where they are provided.

- The school includes education on healthier eating and basic food safety practices in the taught curriculum.

A Year 4 class benefiting from the free fruit and vegetable scheme, devised recipes from their favourite fruits and vegetables and then sent them home to their families in the form of a recipe book. Parents were encouraged to try making the new recipes at home and record as a family what they thought about the recipe, fill in the return sheet and send it back to school with their child. Parents were also encouraged to come into the school to cook the recipes with children and an intergenerational cooking event was held whereby children, their parents and grandparents got together to look at healthy eating over the generations. Evaluations undertaken by the school showed that parents felt more involved in school life and that two-way communication between home and school had improved; some parents even commented that the recipes were now a regular teatime meal in their household.

Physical Activity

Physical activity is something one does. It is about any body movement using muscles and expending energy, such as exercise or a structured, planned physical activity. Physical activity purports many benefits including improved psychological wellbeing, increased self-esteem, improved health and enhanced co-operation and team skills. Participation in physical activity can be adventurous and stimulating; it can often provide a challenge and can allow a young person to explore their environment and develop individual potential.

In a survey of 587 primary schools (Central Council for Physical Recreation and The Times Educational Supplement) it was found that one in six children leave primary school unable to swim. This is despite a three-year government campaign to raise standards. Teachers reported that it is a lack of money, facilities, and time that limits their ability to provide children with sufficient lessons. Teachers and sportsmen say findings have worrying implications for children's safety as well as for Britain's sporting hopes, for example drowning is the third most common cause of death for under 16's with 50 fatalities every year.

This decline in physical activity can be attributed to our increasing sedentary lifestyles, fast foods and the development of home entertainment. It is important for schools to encourage healthy habits and develop a positive attitude to exercise.

- The school has a whole-school approach to the promotion of physical activity.

- The school offers all pupils, whatever their age or ability, a minimum of two hours physical activity a week within and outside the National Curriculum.

- The school is aware of a range of relevant initiatives and networks and takes advantage of appropriate opportunities to promote and develop physical activity.

- The school encourages its staff, pupils, parents/carers and other adults, for example, sports development officers, to become involved in promoting physical activity and develop their skills, abilities and understanding through appropriate training.

Case-study

Schools are increasingly expanding the range of physical activities available to children in school. One school commissioned an external fitness company to run circuit training classes at lunch-time for pupils and then after school for pupils and parents. The classes involved very loud popular music, which was found to initially be one of the major attractions for pupils joining in. However, pupils soon began to ask for the classes, they said they began to see sport in a different way and enjoyed the range of different physical activities that the instructor asked them to do. Another school ran a sponsored skipping marathon; the aim was to have ten people at any one time skipping for a week. Pupils and parents were asked to nominate themselves for one to two fifteen minute stints over the week; the skippers continually rotated over the course of the week and raised over £100.00, which was used to buy some new outdoor playtime equipment for the school.

Personal Safety

Teaching pupils to value themselves, others and their environment can only help to create a more positive safer, place for us all to live. There is an obvious difference between feeling safe and being safe. Feeling safe has already been covered in the emotional health section; being safe requires adopting a responsible attitude whereby everyone is aware of their rights and responsibilities and that they take responsibility for themselves and others.

This requires the whole school community to play a part in developing and maintaining a positive school culture and incorporating a sense of ownership and pride about their school.

This can be achieved when schools develop policy and practice that ensures the safety of the whole school community. For example, schools need policies on first-aid, the administration of medicines and on health and safety. Policies need to have clearly defined roles and responsibilities. Specific rules need to be developed for the whole school, for classrooms, staff rooms and school grounds (such as the grounds are free of litter and graffiti). The school needs a security system to ensure the physical safety of people; school toilets need to have locks, toilet paper, hot water, and paper towels. Furthermore, issues of fire, water and road safety form part of the school's programme as do the school's maintenance of playgrounds, buildings and equipment. All these aspects build up the feeling of safety in staff and children in school.

National Healthy School Standard, DfEE, 1999b

- The school has an identified health and safety representative and regularly conducts risk assessments.

- Members of the whole school community are aware of their roles and responsibilities in ensuring that the school is a healthy and safe environment that includes addressing child protection issues through the curriculum, and having clearly defined procedures for responding to incidents.

- The school provides opportunities for all pupils to develop health skills in relation to first-aid.

- The school provides a healthy and safe playground, which addresses issues of sun safety, has a quiet area and lunch-time supervisors trained in dealing with bullying and organising play activities.

- The school encourages its staff and pupils to consider cycling and walking to and from school and provides training in safety and security supported by safer travel policies.

Case-study

A safety day was organised by one school to help explore all the dangers children may be exposed to in their everyday lives, how they could keep themselves safe and who could help them keep safe. A range of agencies came to the school including the emergency services, environmental

Continued...

projects and road safety groups. Over the course of the day a range of exciting workshops were run that provided interactive activities for pupils and parents to join in together. Lots of photos were taken over the course of the day to make a display board and leaflet on safety.

Other schools are using the concept of the walking bus to promote safety on the way to school; it has also been used by many to reduce bullying on the buses and enhance physical activity. Children are encouraged to walk to school using various routes. An adult leader will meet the children at a named location at a named time, they will then proceed to walk a planned route to school; on the way there are 'bus stops' where pupils can be at certain times to meet up with and join onto the human walking bus. Adults from the school or parents/carers are usually required to staff each of the bus stops and be involved in the walk to school.

Sex and Relationships Education

The sensitive nature of sex and relationships can often deter us from teaching effective Sex and Relationships Education (SRE). However, the rise in teenage pregnancies, sexually transmitted diseases, reported incidents of domestic violence and poor sexual health demonstrates the importance of providing children and young people with the information and skills to develop and maintain healthy safer relationships.

SRE can be addressed through a whole-school policy that allows for consultation with staff, parents and the community to develop an effective confidentiality policy, clear guidelines for child protection issues and the support, appropriate resources and training to help staff deliver SRE with confidence. Further, in order for schools to provide pupils with knowledge of and access to relevant support and information about local sexual health and support services there needs to be a planned programme of SRE addressing issues of positive/safer relationships, sexuality, parenting and responsibility. SRE needs also to present facts, develop skills and explore attitudes.

National Healthy School Standard, DfEE, 1999b

- The school has a policy which is owned and implemented by all members of the school including pupils and parents and which is delivered in partnership with local health and support services.

- The school has a planned sex and relationships education programme (including information, social skills development and values clarification) which identifies learning outcomes, appropriate to pupils' age, ability, gender and level of maturity and which is based on pupils' needs assessment and knowledge of vulnerable pupils.

- Staff have a sound basic knowledge of sex and relationships issues and are confident in their skills to teach sex education and discuss sex and relationships.

- Staff have an understanding of the role of schools in contributing to the reduction of unwanted teenage conceptions and the promotion of sexual health.

Case-study

Depending on the age of the children the learning around SRE is quite different; at Key Stage 1 many schools are now holding more Circle Time discussions around friendships and relationships to introduce the concept early on. One school uses a life like doll and pupils are encouraged to be their friend for the day. Throughout the course of the day the pupils with the doll have to ensure that their new friend feels welcome and able to join in on class activities. Pupils are encouraged to take the doll home to think about how friendships out of school might be different. After a day of being a friend pupils are encouraged to feed back to the class using the sentence: 'One way I was friendly was...' The school believes this has helped promote friendships and pro-social behaviour in the school by encouraging social learning from an early age.

Links with Emotional Health and Wellbeing

Mental Health

The word 'mental' is a very strong and powerful word with many connotations. Mental may be seen to mean madness, people who are very ill, someone who has a lack of control or someone who is violent, abusive and dangerous. Action for Sick Children (Kurtz, 1992) gives the following definition of mental health problems in children and young people:

Abnormalities of emotions, behaviour or social relationships sufficiently marked or prolonged to cause suffering or risk to optimal development in the child or distress or disturbance in the family or community.

Whist this may appear to be an all encompassing definition of the term mental health it is important to be clear that there are differing degrees of disturbance along a continuum of mental health. These can range from mild problems, which a child might be able to work through themselves, to severe illness which requires specialist treatment and possibly hospitalisation. Wired for Health (www.wiredforhealth.gov.uk) define four terms to help put the wider picture of mental health into context.

1. Mental health problems: This refers to a broad range of less serious emotional and behavioural difficulties, covering stress, sadness, anger etc. These vary in the level of distress they cause and the extent to which they interfere with everyday living. Many of these problems pass with time, whilst others require additional help over and above what can ordinarily be provided by carers, relatives and friends or through a GP, a teacher, social workers and others.

2. Mental health disorders: This refers to conditions that are more severe, extreme or distressing and which cause serious interference with everyday life and persist over weeks and months. These disorders are not likely to get better without some specialist help.

3. Mental health disorders can also be referred to as psychiatric disorders: Examples of such disorders are depression, attention deficit hyperactivity disorder (ADHD), conduct disorders and obsessive compulsive disorders.

4. Mental illness: This is the serious end of the spectrum. It refers to very severe mental disturbance which causes great distress and confusion for the young people themselves and those around them. Examples of mental illness are schizophrenia and other psychotic disorders, serious depressive illness and anorexia nervosa.

Put simply, mental health is what it says it is – health of the mind. This means the way we feel, think, perceive and make sense of the world. Children's mental health is much more than the absence of illness, it is about physical and emotional health and wellbeing, about having the strength and capacity to live a full and creative life, and also the flexibility to deal with its unpredictability.

Mental health is about maintaining a good level of personal and social functioning. For children and young people, this means getting on with others, both peers and adults, participating in educative and other social activities, and having a positive self-esteem. Mental health is about coping and adjusting to the demands of growing up. It does not all happen at one point in time and appears to result from an interactive process to which we can all contribute, based on the child's environmental, social and cultural context. (DfES, 2003)

From the angle of this book the term emotional health and wellbeing is applied as a means of maintaining good mental health. What this does not mean is that we are expecting schools to be responsible for treating mental illnesses and disorders and coping, preventing and addressing mental illness in their school. However, schools do have a responsibility to protect and contribute towards a positive state of mental health and act when there are issues arising in their pupils that can be attributed to mental health. What you will see from the next section is that we all need to take care of our emotional health and that by developing a positive outlook on life, about ourselves, the way we feel, think and in the choices we make, we are better equipped to deal with what life throws at us. This in turn, for example, may prevent a build-up of stress or anxiety, thus in the long run reduce the chance of mental health problems developing.

Feelings and Emotional Literacy

Feelings can be emotional (i.e. happy, sad, angry) or physical (i.e. hot, pain, cold). Feelings exist for a reason as Susan Greenfield (2000) states '...our emotions are what make life worth living'. Emotions make up the internal driving force that shapes our experiences and motivates us to behave in certain ways (Long, 1999). Emotions give our lives meaning, they drive us, they help us to learn, they help us survive, they help us interact with and understand others. How we feel is interlinked with how we behave and how we think, thus if we are able to recognise and understand our emotions and effectively handle, respond and express them we are better placed to think more positively about situations and about ourselves and in turn make better decisions and choices about our life.

The concept of emotional literacy is not new, and involves being able to identify, accept, manage and healthily express the full range of feelings. Our physical and emotional health depends on our level of emotional literacy. Our emotions have a dramatic impact on both our physiological state and on our ability to think clearly and learn easily, as well as the behaviour choices that we make.

However, feelings do not follow rules and we are often caught by surprise with our own feelings. All feelings are valid and they contain important information, for example, comfort, pain, safety, trust. It is important to stress that feelings are not good or bad; they are not right or wrong. When something happens we have an internal response to the stimulus and a feeling is triggered, we cannot stop the feeling it is simply there and we cannot choose how we are going to feel in certain situations: we simply feel and then act on our feeling. The choice arrives with the action; at this stage we have a number of choices available about how we respond to the feeling that has emerged.

We often label the range of emotions that exist as positive and negative, however, this is not healthy. All feelings exist for a reason, and whilst it may not be pleasant to feel and experience sadness for example, this does not mean that sadness is negative or bad. We are experiencing that feeling for a reason, whether it is a way of helping us address a painful and upsetting situation or that it helps us recognise something we need to do or change – it helps us respond.

Emotional Health and Wellbeing

Emotional health and wellbeing is about how we feel, think and behave, it is about an individual's capacity to recognise, understand and effectively manage and express feelings and show concern for the feelings of others and respond to them in a mutually supportive environment. It is also about self – self-esteem, self-identity, self-worth and self-respect – and about an individual having the ability to make informed decisions about their lives. How we feel about others, our environment and ourselves plays a vital role in creating and maintaining healthy relationships and influences the strength of those relationships. How we feel about others and ourselves is also directly related to the values and attitudes contained within our social groups, our ability to respond and make safe choices and the self-confidence we have to learn, grow and care for others and ourselves. How we feel about ourselves, others and the world around us, affects the way we respond and cope to all that life has to throw at us.

The BBC website (www.bbc.co.uk) states that in reality nobody feels blissfully happy, thinks positive thoughts, and behaves sensibly all the time – but if you're in a pretty good state of mind generally, it's much easier to enjoy life. Of course, there are times when it's natural to feel sad or anxious – when you've suffered a loss, for example, or if you have to adjust to sudden, unexpected change. But if your mental balance is basically good, you're likely to cope better in a crisis and recover more quickly and more fully.

Looking after your state of mind is as important as taking care of your body, yet most of us manage our physical health far better than our emotional health. As soon as we feel a physical ache or pain we generally try to do something about it, but when we find ourselves feeling very low, or stressed and anxious, we tend to think it's just part and parcel of life and don't do anything to improve the situation.

All children have their ups and downs and go through a range of thoughts and feelings as they grow up. As we know, growing up can be stressful, but with back-up from those around them, most children cope well enough. However, some can't cope and become overwhelmed by their misery, anger or fear, and this is when all kinds of problems can arise. It is this group of children which probably needs some specialist help. Without this help these children run the risk of developing more serious problems (www.wiredforhealth.gov.uk).

'Mind' (2003) report that in 1999 the estimated population of the UK was 59.5 million. Children aged up to 16 made up 20.4% of the population, and those aged 16-24 made up 11% of the population. Research from the Office of National Statistics has shown that 20% of the nation's children suffer some degree of mental or emotional problem and at least a third of these experience continuing problems as adults. For example, 7% of inner city 3 year olds experience moderate to severe problems, while more minor problems affect a further 15%, and 35% of physically abused children will develop a psychiatric problem (The Child Psychotherapy Trust).

Making the link between mental health and emotional health is easy. We all need to maintain positive mental health and to do this we need to have good physical health (free from disease and illness), good emotional health (that is, be emotionally literate) and have a good sense of wellbeing (self-esteem, confidence and sense of worth). This will give us the strength and capacity to live a full and creative life, the flexibility to deal with its unpredictability and the ability to avoid mental health problems, mental illness and mental disorders that may result as a consequence.

Improving the mental health, and maintaining good emotional health and a sense of wellbeing in children and young people, is particularly important because mental health problems in childhood and adolescence can compound each other and may affect school, family and social life with serious consequences in present and later life. The relationships that children and young people have with family members, friends, schools and others, have great significance in their lives. When these relationships are happy and fulfilling they can be a source of support and friendship. Negative or abusive relationships are very damaging and cause much pain both at the time and in the future. Parents and their children will experience conflict and arguments in the natural course of their relationship; this is to be expected. However in some cases poor (or no) communication, verbal or physical violence, abuse and other factors may mean that a child or young person experiences mental distress as well as having no effective and supportive relationships to help them through problems they may encounter. (Mind, 2003)

If a child has poor relationships at school with peers or with teachers this can have long-term effects on relationships as well as immediate consequences on their education. Duck (1991) has shown that the presence of a close intimate relationship with members of our peer group can fend off stress. Faulkner and Miell (1993) have found that gaining peer acceptance and interacting successfully with others is important not only for the success of the period of school transition itself but also for later school adjustment. Children who are initially rejected by their peers seem to hold more negative attitudes to school, have fewer friends and have more adjustment problems several months and even years later (Cole and Dodge, 1988; Parker and Asher, 1987). Cowie and Pechereck (1994) in considering social relationships, believe that children who are neglected by their peers, especially if the situation continues throughout school, may be timid or socially unskilled which in turn causes unhappiness, loneliness and affects the ability to form close friendships.

It is essential that time is spent allowing the whole school community to build a deep and positive sense of wellbeing and a strong emotional self to help us face life's challenges with confidence, whilst remaining within a nurturing environment that respects everyone's right to feel safe.

Bullying

'Mind' report that one in four primary school children and one in ten secondary school children are bullied. In recent years bullying has been recognised as a serious problem that cannot be tolerated in schools and many schools have taken active steps to tackle it. Bullying always needs to be taken seriously: there are cases where a bullied child has been too scared to discuss the problem with anyone, or has not been listened to or supported when they have, and has in the end committed suicide in despair of getting any help. (www.mind.org.uk)

Evidence suggests that consideration for the physical and emotional wellbeing of pupils and implementing preventative work around bullying behaviour can create a safer school environment as well as raise academic achievement. For this to be accomplished the whole school needs to be proactive in creating and sustaining a safer environment for all.

Bullying plays a large part when considering emotional health and wellbeing of children and young people. It is prevalent in our society and in our schools and can have dramatic and long-term effects on young people as well as their future lives as adults.

Stress

> Stress is the way our body responds physically and/or psychologically when we are in situations where we feel under threat but are not actually in any immediate danger, the response is one very similar to that of fear, the difference being that when we are scared or fearful we usually have cause to be concerned about our wellbeing or safety.

> (The Stress Consultancy)

Stress can result from negative experiences such as bereavements, divorce, illness and accidents but positive experiences like marriage, moving home or new jobs can also be very stressful. Stress in itself is not necessarily harmful – we need goals and challenges in life or we get bored. We need a degree of stress in our lives to help us achieve our goals. Some people can tolerate all sorts of major life changes without feeling pressured, while others find it difficult to cope when life gets stressful.

Too much stress, however, can be damaging and can lead to illness and restrictions in our lives. For example, stress is a well-known trigger for depression and it can also lead to related diseases such as asthma, hypertension and ulcers. Some people who are stressed suffer from anxiety, panic attacks and hyperventilation and others respond with obsessive thoughts and behaviours and may suffer from a variety of phobias.

There is a strong link between emotional health and wellbeing, mental health and stress, and from this description alone you can see why it is important to identify the stress factors in your life and do everything you can to minimise them. It is also important to recognise stress in schools, both in staff and pupils. Smith et al (2000) state that, '42% of teachers reported that they were highly stressed. This compares to an average of 20% of workers (in all occupations) reporting high or very high levels of stress at work.' Many different situations can lead to stress at work, including relationships with colleagues, an unsupportive boss, lack of consultation and communication, too much interference with your private, social or family life, too much or too little to do, too much pressure, unrealistic deadlines, work that is too difficult or not demanding enough, lack of control over the way the work is done, poor working conditions, being in the wrong job, feeling undervalued, insecurity and the threat of unemployment.

It is reported on the BBC website (www.bbc.co.uk/healthconditions/mental_health/emotion_stress.shtml) that work-related stress is the second biggest occupational health problem in the UK and an estimated half a million employees say they are experiencing work-related stress, including anxiety and depression. However, because there is still an unjust stigma attached to mental health problems, employees are often reluctant to seek help in case they are perceived as 'not being able to cope'. When people feel under impossible pressure at work, they tend to work harder and harder to try to close the gap between what they are achieving and what they think they should be achieving. They stop taking breaks and often lose touch with their own needs.

It is not just adults who can become stressed, it can affect children and young people too. The concerns of SATs, exams and coursework, homework, fashion, friendships, sexuality, issues at home and in the community and so on, can put great feelings of pressure on children and young people and lead to the onset of stress related conditions.

It is important to take action to relieve damaging stress before it affects physical or mental health and have strategies to prevent stress arising. It is essential for schools to recognise and provide staff and pupils alike with the avenues to get help and support if they feel stressed, to avoid stress in staff and children through good communication, avoid burdening staff and pupils and to create an ethos that promotes emotional health and wellbeing and does not give a message that stress is a sign of weakness. A good school may even be proactive in dealing with and managing stress in their pupils and staff by providing strategies to recognise, manage and deal with stress should it arise.

Self-esteem

By self-esteem we refer to the evaluation that the individual makes and customarily maintains with regard to himself; it expresses an attitude of approval or disapproval and indicates the extent to which the individual believes himself to be capable, significant, successful and worthy. So self-esteem is the personal judgement of worthiness that is expressed in the attitude the individual holds toward himself and the extent to which he accepts or approves of himself. (Coopersmith, 1967)

Definitions of self-esteem can vary somewhat, but all agree that, 'high self-esteem means that we appreciate ourselves and our personal worth. More specifically, it means we have a positive attitude, we evaluate ourselves highly, we are convinced of our own abilities, we see ourselves as competent and in control of our own lives and able to do what we want.' (www.bbc.co.uk). In making the link between self-esteem and emotional health and wellbeing one could say that if we have a positive wellbeing we will have high self-esteem, similarly low self-esteem can be equated to poor wellbeing.

How much we like ourselves can be an overall judgement or it can relate to specific areas in our lives, i.e. we can have a high opinion of ourselves but dislike certain characteristics. Our self-esteem can be regarded as how we evaluate our self-image, that is, how much we like the kind of person we think we are. Self-esteem will also be partly determined by how much our self-image (the way in which we would describe ourselves; the kind of person we think we are) differs from our ideal self (the kind of person – part or whole – we would like to be). The greater the gap between our self-image and our ideal self, the lower our self-esteem. Low self-esteem could thus be described as disliking, judging or rejecting parts of yourself and high self-esteem liking yourself for who you are.

In education, the issue of a child's self-esteem is a vitally important consideration. Self-esteem affects a child's behaviour in all aspects of school life including academic and social. Children with high positive regard are more likely to achieve academically and less likely to be in trouble than children with poor or low self-regard (Bliss, T. and Tetley, J. 1993). Children with low self-esteem look for information to confirm their poor view of themselves and behave in a manner, which is consistent with this view. Examples of such behaviour traits include:

- fear of failure – finds it difficult to try new strategies or will simply refuse to 'have a go', will often destroy work even if it is good or avoid work and use delaying tactics

- feel inadequate, useless, incompetent, unpopular and/or of little use – lack in confidence and are unsure of themselves, find it difficult to make decisions, reluctant to join in

- appear anxious and/or depressed – reluctant to join in, may become socially isolated

- rigid in his/her thinking – negative self-talk about oneself, looks for proof of negatives, sets unrealistic goals for oneself that are either too high or too low

- feeling uncomfortable with praise – unable to or finds it hard to accept praise, feel unworthy of praise, feel no one likes them

- unable to ask for needs to be met

- more disruptive – personal feelings of frustration and anger, attention seeking

- critical and jealous of others
- inability to be warm and affectionate – rarely laughs or smiles
- being negative about self, particularly in comparison with others – puts him/herself down, negative self-talk.

Burt et al (1999) suggest that to value ourselves we need to feel some mastery over ourselves and experience success. However, to get children with low self-esteem to 'hear' and believe positive messages about themselves can be a challenging task.

The self-esteem of adults in school is just as important as the pupils. Staff with a low self-esteem may not feel confident about their lesson delivery or they may lack confidence in dealing with difficult situations in the classroom. Generally if someone is not feeling good about themselves this may not only affect them, their work and their life but also their relationship with others. Once again it is possible to see the immediate link that self-esteem has with emotional health and wellbeing, thus any school looking at developing the emotional health and wellbeing theme would need to take into consideration how self-esteem of pupils and of staff is developed and maintained within their school.

The Emotional Health and Wellbeing Theme of the National Healthy Schools Standard

Schools need to create an environment that enables pupils and staff to:

- work and learn
- develop positive attitudes and values that help them to get on with each other
- be physically, mentally and socially healthy
- be happy with who they are and the contribution they are making to the life of the school and their community.

Feeling good about yourself, being happy and healthy, is linked to levels of high self-esteem. High self-esteem is well documented to be a great influence on academic achievement, success and having the ability to make positive life choices that develop and maintain healthy, balanced relationships.

The Emotional Health and Wellbeing Theme recognises that prevention is better than cure. It is important to be part of the solution rather than part of the problem. By overlooking emotional health and wellbeing we could risk costs of up to billions of pounds for the UK in sickness mental disorders, anxiety, depression therefore it makes good sense to send our children out into the world emotionally healthy and with a highly developed sense of wellbeing.

What follows is a selection of good practice that fulfils the Healthy School Standard, which schools working on emotional health and wellbeing may wish to develop.

Chapter Two

Developing the Emotional Health and Wellbeing (Including Bullying) Standard

The Process

Once your school has decided to develop the Emotional Health and Wellbeing NHSS Theme (which may have been identified through a larger healthy schools audit on all themes) there is a logical process for the school to take:

Step One

Make a decision on the theme(s) you wish to address and contact your LEA healthy school team for help, support, advice and guidance. Register for the NHSS.

Step Two

Allocate a healthy schools co-ordinator in your school and develop a task group to help take the theme forward in the school.

Step Three

Undertake an emotional health and wellbeing (including bullying) audit.

Step Four

Feed back findings.

Step Five

Develop an emotional health and wellbeing action plan as part of the school development plan (SDP) – the action plan may need to be endorsed by your healthy schools team within the LEA.

Step Six

Implement the action plan and gather evidence of its implementation.

Step Seven

Submit evidence for accreditation.

Step Eight

Receive accreditation.

Step Nine

Celebrate.

Step Ten

Review practice regularly.

Step One: Make a Decision on the Theme

The NHSS themes are fully outlined in Chapter One, there are eight to choose from:

1. Personal, Social and Health Education

2. Citizenship

3. Drug Education (including alcohol and tobacco)

4. Emotional Health and Wellbeing (including bullying)

5. Healthy eating

6. Physical Activity

7. Safety

8. Sex and Relationship Education.

It is not compulsory to address one theme; you may decide to address two or three together.

In making a decision on which Healthy Schools themes to take forward one school decided to review all their strengths and weaknesses, and identify any links that there may be to the themes under Healthy Schools. The schools pupils' attendance was low, staff absence was high, staff stress was high, retention of staff was poor and there were a high number of reported incidents of bullying. Following consultation with pupils and staff it was decided that the theme of emotional health, wellbeing and bullying may impact on these areas and give both pupils and staff a boost.

Step Two: Allocate a Co-ordinator and Develop a Task Group

Allocate a Project Co-ordinator

It is recommended that for the success of the scheme a member of staff or a group of staff be assigned as healthy schools programme co-ordinator or manager. These staff will need to be allocated sufficient time to dedicate to the implementation and daily management of the theme.

The role of the project co-ordinator(s) will be:

- to implement and establish the programme
- to oversee the devising and implementation of an emotional health and wellbeing action plan
- to promote the programme and engage support among school staff, senior management, governors, parents and pupils
- to be involved in any external training that may be required
- to supervise or help co-supervise teaching staff or facilitators delivering the emotional health and wellbeing curriculum and implementing actions from the plan
- to be one of a number of points of contact for questions
- to organise events around the theme
- to co-ordinate any additional resources coming into the school or new programmes running in the school to support the scheme

- to review, monitor, evaluate the programme and implement change where necessary.

While a great degree of time and energy may be required to set up new procedures and implement the curriculum, when one sees the effects that the system can have not only on pupils but on staff, parents, carers and the whole school community, the value of the investment of time in the programme soon becomes apparent.

For whoever oversees the implementation of the healthy school standard the main concern is commitment and motivation to support the project and the young people involved.

Developing a task group

When a school is aspiring to make changes to its ethos and methods of support, it is implicit that these changes become integrated in to all parts of school life. Concepts and methods of working embraced by some members of school staff and not others give an inconsistent message and can be damaging.

Imagine that a child enters school in the morning and is greeted by a member of staff who acknowledges the importance of the emotional health of all pupils and is therefore friendly, welcoming and talkative with the young person as they arrive, immediately the child will feel valued and important, have a sense that they belong and the school has an interest in them as a person and not just as a pupil. This child then goes along to their classroom where again their class teacher is friendly, welcoming and works within clear and consistent boundaries. Again the child feels listened to, supported and cared for and feels able to address any concerns they have with their teacher.

Imagine now that the child moves into a literacy lesson with a different teacher or starts to work in a small group with a classroom assistant and is dictated to about where to sit and who to sit next to, told that their opinion is irrelevant today, that they are to listen and not be heard. Imagine that the child is struggling with the work and when asks for help is presented with negative non-verbal behaviour by the teacher or classroom assistant. Suddenly that sense of belonging, that feeling of self-worth, of safety and of being valued has disappeared.

How this pupil will feel by the end of the school day may be dependent on the actions, reactions, behaviours and communication with others in the school, other pupils, other teachers, the lunch-time staff, the head teacher and so on.

We cannot guarantee that all our interactions at all times will be the best and we all have times when we wish we could turn back the clock and approach a situation differently. However, if everyone in the school plays a part in creating a warm, caring, friendly, respectful and valuing ethos each child will have the opportunity at school to enable them to develop in a emotionally healthy way.

The message here is that when we are creating an ethos that aims to develop all our pupils in the school into emotionally healthy adults the planning for this cannot come from one part of the school alone. A task group will need to be developed that represents a cross section of the whole school community. Members of the task group for example may include:

- named healthy school co-ordinator (for the school)
- pupils
- parents/carers
- governors
- school support staff
- teaching staff
- senior staff/SMT
- parent helpers
- education and behaviour support staff
- strand leader for emotional health and wellbeing with the LEA healthy schools team
- SENCO/EBD co-ordinator
- PSHE/Citizenship co-ordinator
- pastoral manager.

It is essential to the success of the initiative that a whole-school approach is adopted. All staff need to be well informed about the aims and rationale of the 'healthy schools emotional health and wellbeing, including bullying, theme' and of how it is to be developed and run. The backing of senior management, all school staff, governors, parents, carers and pupils will ensure that the programme becomes an integrated part of the school system.

Once in operation the programme may cause some minor disturbances, i.e. planning the lessons and preparing for small group work, so it is essential that staff not only agree to this but also are clear about the long-term benefits to pupils and the whole school. To ensure a whole-school approach is adopted a number of things can be done:

- Present the concept of the emotional health and wellbeing theme at a staff meeting (provide an information sheet to all staff).

- Provide an information sheet or do a verbal presentation to governors.

- Send letters to parents/carers of all pupils.

- Incorporate the emotional health and wellbeing theme and its benefits into school policy.

- Advertise, celebrate and inform the whole school community about what is happening through school or local community magazines or newsletters.

Once the scheme has been established communication about the programme needs to continue with parents, carers, pupils, senior management, teachers and governors. This can be done via some of these suggested avenues. Another suggestion and easy mechanism is to have a designated notice board in the school where updates, stories, work from the emotional health and wellbeing curriculum and theme in general and feedback about the effects of the curriculum can be continually displayed in and around the school.

Case-study

In many schools the obvious choice for the healthy schools co-ordinator is the current PSHCE co-ordinator, a member of the pastoral staff or the SENCO. One school decides to take a different approach and post an open invitation for all staff to apply for the role, both teaching and non-teaching. This method led to a school governor taking up the role as healthy schools co-ordinator; in this instance the person had more time and was very keen and motivated to facilitate the activities and inspire the whole school community into achieving their healthy schools accreditation.

Once the co-ordinator was allocated the school used the same process to establish a task group; an advertisement was put out to pupils, parents, teachers, external agencies, community members and governors. There was a great response and as a result the task group had a sense of ownership over the task and a huge sense of commitment to making it happen.

Step Three: Needs Analysis – An Emotional Health and Wellbeing Audit

The audit tool is to help keep your school focused on the theme of emotional health and to ensure development is made on a 'whole school' level. The audit tool represents the ten areas where the school needs to provide evidence to show that they have embedded the ethos of emotional health in the school. As noted earlier, in order for a school to achieve the NHSS award they need to ensure a holistic approach is adopted and that they embrace a whole-school approach to change, development and support, thus evidence for change needs to be evident in:

1. Leadership, management and managing change

2. Policy development

3. Curriculum planning, finding resources and working with external agencies

4. Teaching and learning

5. School culture and environment

6. Giving pupils a voice

7. Provision of pupils' support services

8. Staff professional development needs, health and welfare

9. Partnerships with parents, carers and local communities

10. Assessing recording and reporting pupils' achievements.

(National Health School Standard, DfEE, 1999b)

By undertaking the audit, the school identifies areas of existing strength and areas where there are weaknesses across the school with regards to emotional health and wellbeing.

The audit designed by the authors of this book comprises nine sections. Whilst the audit sections do not parallel in name the ten areas listed above, all elements of the ten statements are covered by the audit. The sections are:

1. Pupil Participation

2. Health and Wellbeing of Staff

3. Parent and Community Partnership

4. School Policies

5.   Developing PSHE and Citizenship

6.   School Environment and Ethos

7.   Equal Opportunities

8.   Pupil Support, Guidance and Welfare

9.   Leadership and Management.

Each section comprises six statements, making a total of 54 statements. These statements are the quality standards that need to be met in order to achieve the national healthy school standard.

It is advised that the allocated healthy schools co-ordinator ensures the completion of the audit. It is suggested that the audit is used with a cross section of people from the school and the school community. The person taking the lead will need to approach groups such as:

- pupils
- parents/carers
- governors
- teaching school staff
- non-teaching school staff
- senior management
- community members
- external agencies supporting the school
- regular school visitors.

The audit can be given to these people individually to complete in questionnaire form or you may wish to interview groups to gain a consensus response. Whichever form is chosen a representative proportion of each of these groups will need to be involved in the audit process. This will ensure that the audit is a true reflection of the whole school community giving a more detailed analysis of the school's needs. Alternatively on a smaller scale it is possible for the task group to complete the audit so long as the group represents a cross section of the school and community.

The collection of information will take no longer than an hour for each group, or an individual, to complete as a questionnaire. When rating the statement the group or individual will need to decide on a response (this will be a collective response based on a consensus if you are interviewing a group) and give each statement a rating between 0 and 3, where:

0 = The issue has not been identified in the school and nothing is happening.

1 = There is an awareness of the issue but nothing is being done about it.

2 = The issue has been identified and the school has made a start in addressing it.

3 = This is normal practice, i.e. it is identified, addressed, regularly reviewed and updated.

The audit exists in only one form, it may be necessary to adapt wording for specific groups i.e. parents, carers, pupils, community.

Case-study

One school, which was very committed to gaining the views of all members of the local school community, took an in-depth approach to getting feedback and responses to audit questions; this was based on their prior experience that simply sending out questionnaires did not work.

With regards to pupils, time was allocated in school for the class teacher to work with their class over a lesson to take feedback from small groups. To do this each class in turn was given the support of two classroom assistants and the behaviour support assistant. In groups of eight pupils were asked to rate the questions; wording was adapted depending on the age group of the children, but the context of the question was not modified. By the end of the week all pupils in the school had inputted into the questionnaire.

Parents, community members and external agencies were invited in for small group discussion and feedback. To entice these groups into the school free raffle tickets were advertised with prizes of either a stereo (third prize), a DVD player (second prize) or a family ticket to the local football match (first prize); the school sought these as donations from local companies. The attraction of the raffle brought in many parents and community members and an extensive range of views was gained.

During a governor meeting the audit was the agenda; ensuring again that the view of all governors was gained. The same was done at a staff meeting, whereby the meeting was cancelled but teachers were asked to complete the questionnaire during that allocated time.

Continued...

To ensure that everyone who wanted to give feedback had done so, the school also left blank questionnaires in reception and a postbox was put up so that people could bring back their questionnaires anonymously should they wish to.

Quality Standards for Emotional Health and Wellbeing (Including Bullying)

Emotional Health and Wellbeing Audit

Section 1: Pupil Participation

Statement	Rating	Comments
1. There is an avenue for pupils' opinions and ideas about the school to be heard.		
2. Pupils' opinions and ideas about the school are acted on.		
3. Pupils take part in policy development (i.e. policies for bullying, behaviour, drugs, sex and relationships).		
4. Pupils take part in the development of school practice (i.e. school rules, vision statement, timetabling, opening and closing hours, extra curricula).		
5. Pupils take responsibility for the school environment (i.e. litter pickers, create displays).		
6. Pupil feedback and/or evaluation about the school is regularly sought on a range of issues.		

0 = The issue has not been identified in the school and nothing is happening.
1 = There is an awareness of the issue but nothing is being done about it.
2 = The issue has been identified and the school has made a start in addressing it.
3 = This is normal practice i.e. it is identified, addressed, regularly reviewed and updated.

Other comments on the section:

Section 2: Health and Wellbeing of Staff

Statement	Rating	
7. The school identifies the health and welfare needs of all its school staff.		
8. All school staff have their training and development needs met including development of knowledge in emotional health and wellbeing, including bullying.		
9. All school staff have a mechanism of support that is accessible, confidential and addresses emotional health needs (i.e. supervision, staff support teams).		
10. All school staff are aware of how to get their needs met (i.e. they are aware of the processes and procedures).		
11. The school actively seeks ways to develop the skills of staff and staff self-esteem and self-confidence.		
12. All staff are aware of the procedure to make complaints and grievances.		

0 = The issue has not been identified in the school and nothing is happening.
1 = There is an awareness of the issue but nothing is being done about it.
2 = The issue has been identified and the school has made a start in addressing it.
3 = This is normal practice i.e. it is identified, addressed, regularly reviewed and updated.

Other comments on the section:

Section 3: Parent and Community Partnership

Statement	Rating	Comments
13. There is an avenue for parents' and carers' opinions and ideas about the school to be heard.		
14. Parents'/ carers' opinions and ideas about the school are acted on.		
15. Parents are informed about all school practices and developments.		
16. The school has effective links with their local community.		
17. Parents, carers and the community are involved with emotional health and wellbeing in the school (i.e. curriculum, partnership work).		
18. Parent and community feedback and/or evaluation about the school is regularly sought on a range of issues.		

0 = The issue has not been identified in the school and nothing is happening.
1 = There is an awareness of the issue but nothing is being done about it.
2 = The issue has been identified and the school has made a start in addressing it.
3 = This is normal practice i.e. it is identified, addressed, regularly reviewed and updated.

Other comments on the section:

Section 4: School Policies

Statement	Rating	Comments
19. The school has an up to date Drugs policy that is informed by national guidelines that all school staff and pupils are aware of.		
20. The school has an up to date Sex and Relationship policy that is informed by national guidelines that all school staff and pupil are aware of.		
21. The school has an up to date Child Protection policy that is informed by national guidelines that all school staff and pupils are aware of and includes a nominated CP officer.		
22. The school has an up to date Behaviour policy that is informed by national guidelines that all school staff and pupils are aware of.		
23. The school has a policy that makes reference to emotional health and wellbeing of staff and pupils and that all school staff and pupils are aware of (i.e. behaviour, bullying, equal opportunities).		
24. The school has a policy and code of practice for addressing bullying which is owned, understood and implemented by all of the school community and includes contact with external agencies.		

0 = The issue has not been identified in the school and nothing is happening.
1 = There is an awareness of the issue but nothing is being done about it.
2 = The issue has been identified and the school has made a start in addressing it.
3 = This is normal practice i.e. it is identified, addressed, regularly reviewed and updated.

Other comments on the section.

Section 5: Developing PSHE and Citizenship

Statement	Rating	Comments
25. There is a named PSHE/ Citizenship co-ordinator who has time to plan, review, monitor and evaluate the PSHE and Citizenship curriculum and meet with external agencies and other local schools.		
26. All school staff play a part in the delivery of PSHE and Citizenship and have resources and support to enable them to do this effectively.		
27. The school provides opportunities for pupils to become informed, active and responsible citizens.		
28. The school provides opportunities in all areas of school life for developing and promoting its pupils' personal, social and health needs.		
29. The emotional health curriculum is planned and there is a scheme of work for staff to follow that reflects local and national guidelines.		
30. Staff are generally confident in the implementation of the PSHE and Citizenship syllabus.		

0 = The issue has not been identified in the school and nothing is happening.
1 = There is an awareness of the issue but nothing is being done about it.
2 = The issue has been identified and the school has made a start in addressing it.
3 = This is normal practice i.e. it is identified, addressed, regularly reviewed and updated.

Other comments on the section:

Section 6: School Environment and Ethos

Statement	Rating	Comments
31. The whole-school ethos is one that cares for, develops and supports its pupils, staff, parents, carers and visitors.		
32. The school is welcoming and safe for pupils, parents, carers, staff and visitors.		
33. The school follows up incidents of bullying behaviour.		
34. The school is secure and well maintained providing a physically safe environment (i.e. security).		
35. The school's organisation, culture and ethos support pupils' spiritual, moral, social and cultural development.		
36. The learning environment actively encourages and promotes good emotional health and wellbeing.		

0 = The issue has not been identified in the school and nothing is happening.
1 = There is an awareness of the issue but nothing is being done about it.
2 = The issue has been identified and the school has made a start in addressing it.
3 = This is normal practice i.e. it is identified, addressed, regularly reviewed and updated.

Other comments on the section:

Section 7: Equal Opportunities

Statement	Rating	Comments
37. There is an equal opportunities policy and code of practice for addressing issues that all school staff and pupils are aware of.		
38. School staff has received training in the implementation of equal opportunities.		
39. Everyone in the school demonstrates equal opportunities in their working practice and is able to recognise and celebrate diversity and difference.		
40. Everyone feels they are treated equally.		
41. Diversity is valued and celebrated in the school.		
42. External agencies support the work of specific groups within school (i.e. refugees, travelling children, Looked After Children).		

0 = The issue has not been identified in the school and nothing is happening.
1 = There is an awareness of the issue but nothing is being done about it.
2 = The issue has been identified and the school has made a start in addressing it.
3 = This is normal practice i.e. it is identified, addressed, regularly reviewed and updated.

Other comments on the section:

Section 8: Pupil Support, Guidance and Welfare

Statement	Rating	Comments
43. The school openly addresses issues of emotional health and wellbeing by enabling pupils to understand what they are feeling and by building their confidence to learn.		
44. There is a system for providing confidential support and guidance and pupils are aware of the ways this can be accessed.		
45. Pupils' achievements are recognised and celebrated (i.e. personal and academic achievements).		
46. The school has and continues to create opportunities to develop pupils' self-esteem.		
47. Pupils have access to support and guidance from the LEA and external agencies where required, and the school is aware of the full range of specialist services for emotional health and wellbeing.		
48. The school actively seeks ways to develop the self-esteem, self-worth and self-confidence of pupils.		

0 = The issue has not been identified in the school and nothing is happening.
1 = There is an awareness of the issue but nothing is being done about it.
2 = The issue has been identified and the school has made a start in addressing it.
3 = This is normal practice i.e. it is identified, addressed, regularly reviewed and updated.

Other comments on the section:

Section 9: Leadership and Management

Statement	Rating	Comments
49. The governing body is aware of the responsibility to promote the emotional health and wellbeing of its staff and pupils.		
50. Management ensures that emotional health and wellbeing, including bullying, is addressed within the curriculum and that appropriate resources are available.		
51. Management ensures that there is a whole-school approach to the emotional health and wellbeing of pupils.		
52. The school regularly monitors and evaluates the effectiveness of policy and practice related to emotional health and wellbeing, including bullying (i.e. policies on behaviour, bullying etc.).		
53. The school openly addresses issues of emotional health and wellbeing.		
54. A budget is allocated to the development of work in emotional health and wellbeing, including bullying.		

0 = The issue has not been identified in the school and nothing is happening.
1 = There is an awareness of the issue but nothing is being done about it.
2 = The issue has been identified and the school has made a start in addressing it.
3 = This is normal practice i.e. it is identified, addressed, regularly reviewed and updated.

Other comments on the section:

Scoring the Audit

The audit is grouped into nine sections as follows:

Section	Section content	Questions
1	Pupil Participation	1 - 6
2	Health and Wellbeing of Staff	7 - 12
3	Parent and Community Partnership	13 - 18
4	School Policies	19 - 24
5	Developing PSHE and Citizenship	25 - 30
6	School Environment and Ethos	31 - 36
7	Equal Opportunities	37 - 42
8	Pupil Support, Guidance and Welfare	43 - 48
9	Leadership and Management	49 - 54

Using all the questionnaire responses take an average score of each of the 54 questions. The average needs to be calculated from all the responses irrespective of who completed the questionnaire; do not break them down by parent, community, pupil, staff etc. as your final score needs to reflect a whole-school interpretation. Record the averages into a table such as the one below:

1		7		13		19		25		31		37		43		49	
2		8		14		20		26		32		38		44		50	
3		9		15		21		27		33		39		45		51	
4		10		16		22		28		34		40		46		52	
5		11		17		23		29		35		41		47		53	
6		12		18		24		30		36		42		48		54	

(Numbers correspond to audit question number.)

It may be helpful to plot the scores onto a graph. This will help you identify your areas of strength and areas of weakness and feed back to the school staff visually.

- If the average score is three this is deemed to be strength and does not require action.

- If the score is two this is deemed to be above average and does not require action.

- If the score is one or below, this will need to be considered for action in your plan.

- Scores of zero are deemed to be in need of priority action.

Step Four: Feed Back Findings

Once the audit has been completed it is important to feed back to staff the findings of the audit and explain the next stages in the process. It may be necessary to receive comments on the feedback from staff, governors, pupils and so on if the school feel any further qualitative input would be of use. After the initial feedback has been given it is important to get a whole-school input into developments. There are two options available, firstly that the original task group make decisions on how to respond to the audit and then filter this down to the whole school, or secondly that working groups are developed across the school community to discuss ideas for improving the areas of weakness revealed by the audit and then these ideas are fed into the task group to develop a plan of action. The latter option is ideal as input is gained into school development from across the whole school.

Case-study

One school made feedback a big priority; the task group were given a permanent slot on the school notice board that was displayed in the reception area for everyone to see. All successes and evidence collected appeared on the board and were updated by the task group and school council on a weekly basis. Space was created underneath the board to write comments and new ideas and a postbox was available in the staff room and year group areas. The school also used whole-school assemblies to feed back on activities and progress and to promote new ideas.

Step Five: Develop an Action Plan

Once you have found an average score for each area and question in the audit you will clearly identify the school's areas of strength and the areas in need of improvement. As highlighted previously, any question that has an average of one or below requires action. However if the school has not scored this low on many areas and feels it still needs to develop further in the area of emotional health and wellbeing, including bullying, then scores of two and below can be included into the areas for development. Similarly if the school has scored very low in a wide range of areas, prioritise the actions that are of the lowest score.

Once the key areas for development have been identified the task group need to develop a set of aims and objectives based on moving forward the theme of emotional health throughout the school. The aims need to be a set of overarching accomplishments such as:

- to ensure the whole school is fulfilling their responsibility to developing effective and relevant PSHE and Citizenship that would promote pupils spiritual, moral, social and cultural development and prepare all pupils for the opportunities, responsibilities and experiences of life

- to raise the confidence and capability of all staff to empower pupils, to raise their self-esteem and enable them to make positive life choices

- to increase and sustain partnership working with local agencies and young people's services

- to provide and promote healthier lifestyles for the whole school community.

The objectives are the specifics of what will be seen if the aim was being carried out. For example, if the aim is: to raise the confidence and capability of all staff to empower pupils and to raise their self-esteem and enable them to make positive life choices, the objective or objectives may be:

- to design and deliver an inclusive 'emotional health and wellbeing' programme for the whole school

- to establish and support the roles required for developing and maintaining the programme

- to monitor and evaluate staff personal and professional development and fulfil their emotional health and wellbeing needs.

Some examples of aims and objectives can be seen in the example of a Health Schools Action Plan for Emotional Health and Wellbeing (Including Bullying) at the end of the chapter.

Once the aims and objectives have been devised it is the role of the task group to produce an action plan for the school outlining how the aims and objectives will be carried out. This needs to clearly state:

- what areas are being taken forward (the objective)

- how this will be done (the action needed)

- when it will be done by (a completion date)

- who will lead on the area and who will be involved in its development (the nominated person in the task group to oversee this development and any other people who will be involved such as parents, carers, pupils and class teachers)

- how it will be evidenced (what will be the end result and how will one know that this has been achieved).

Agreeing a Plan of Action

Once the action plan has been developed it should be shared with the whole school community. This may involve feedback at a staff meeting, informing school councils, informing pupils via tutor groups, outlining clearly the developments in the parents newsletter, informing the governors, gaining the support of any agencies or any regular external support you have at the school and so forth. Ensure that everyone is clear what role they have to play on making this work. Once the action plan has been agreed it should be incorporated into the school development plan.

Case-study

One school put on an after school event that brought together children, parents, governors, community members and teachers to help draw up a plan of action. The school's focus was emotional health, wellbeing and bullying and the audit had shown that the areas that needed specific development were support for parents and children and giving pupils a voice.

Those that attended the twilight session were divided into mixed groups of six to eight. A facilitator led the session and took the group through the task step-by-step. The facilitator started by outlining where the school stood with the audit findings and which sections were weak. Next, each group was given a piece of flip-chart paper and asked, 'If you were to wake up tomorrow and this school was operating in the best possible way that it could, with regards to supporting its parents and children, what would be happening?' Each group was asked to spend fifteen minutes recording words, short sentences, pictures and ideas in response to the question.

Continued...

49

After fifteen minutes had passed each group was given a large piece of paper with a picture of a flight of seven stairs on it; on the bottom stair was a description of the current status of the school in the area (i.e. that which was identified as poor on the audit). The groups were asked to stick their pictures, words and sentences onto the top stair and then were given a further fifteen minutes to think about what needed to happen to get from the bottom of the staircase to the top, that is, from the current status to the new improved school. Groups were asked to be as specific as they could about the steps of action that were required to make this progress.

After the end of the session a small buffet was provided for everyone who participated. The task group took away the ideas and used them to compile a more formalised action plan. The school however was safe in the knowledge that the action plan was not merely a set of ideas that were being imposed by senior management, but was in fact owned by the school community themselves. The school believed that the implication of this method is that the pupils, parents, teachers and so forth were more likely to carry out the actions as they were ideas generated from them directly.

Step Six: Implementing the Plan

Once the action plan has been agreed and endorsed by your local healthy school team it is time to start making the changes and implementing the ideas to move the theme forward in the school. It is important to remember that you are not alone. There are many agencies and organisations locally that may be able to help you develop your ideas in the school. For example, if you wish to develop a school council to help give pupils a voice in the school the NSPCC or a representative from your behaviour support team may come in to do the training with the council members, and provide you with help and support in developing the council effectively.

Throughout the period of developing the theme in the school it is important that the school has someone overseeing the changes and/or developments. This may be the role of the healthy schools co-ordinator who was nominated earlier to support the national healthy school status. It may be that different people in the school are allocated different roles and responsibilities for overseeing different aspects of development and/or change in the school.

It is important to be realistic about what you are going to do based on the funds and resources you have available. There is no point, for example, writing into the action plan that you will appoint a qualified school counsellor to provide a confidential service to pupils if there is no money in the budget for new appointments. It may be that you opt instead for a counselling placement of a student on a local counselling course.

It is also important to remember the impact that developments may have on the training needs of staff. It may be, as a result of the changes the school wishes to make, that someone in the school needs intense training on a specific area or that, as a result of development in a policy, all the school staff need training in new information and procedures affecting the school and its pupils.

Finally, it is imperative that all staff are on board with the changes you are making and that they are able to tap into support, if necessary, to help them adapt to new ideas, methods and procedures.

Case-study

Throughout implementing the plan, collecting evidence along the way about how the implementation was being achieved became an activity in itself for one school. They had photographs galore as a result of providing disposable cameras in classrooms for teachers and pupils to record and capture what they were doing. Each class's task was to put together a photograph album of class progress. Classes then voted for the best representation of their activities. All memorabilia were collated into a school scrapbook that consisted of photos, statements, captions, drawings, examples of work and so forth. The scrapbook was then left in reception for all to see.

Step Seven: Submitting the Evidence

To gain National Healthy School Status the school will need to submit evidence that they have reached the aims and objectives laid out in their action plan. Evidence can be varied and may take the form of documented schemes of work, photographs, newsletters, evaluation forms, verbal and written feedback about new developments and/or changes, written or recorded appraisals of the effects given by pupils, staff and/or parents, display boards, leaflets, art work and so on.

You will need to speak to your local healthy school team with the LEA at this stage to ensure that you provide them with the information and evidence that they require to assess you for accreditation.

Case-study

An innovative method of submitting evidence was devised when one school invited their local healthy schools team to attend their school for a day. It began with a tour of the school given by pupils who pointed out displays of their work around the emotional health theme. The team then observed an assembly on feelings lead by Year 6 pupils. Observations of classes formed the remainder of the morning where demonstrations were given around how emotional health had been entwined across the curriculum. The lunch hour was spent with the task group and school council who spoke about their experiences of developing the emotional health, wellbeing and bullying theme and the day ended with a debrief from school staff about how they intended to ensure that progress was sustained and remained an integrated part of school life. Needless to say the school got their award.

Step Eight: Receiving Accreditation

Once you have satisfied the criteria of your local healthy school team they will award you with the national healthy school standard. Having the standard means different things to different authorities, for example, you may be given a logo to use on correspondence from the school to mark the fact you are a healthy school; it may mean that you receive a bursary to support further developments or maintain the status in your school – the result locally of achieving the status will vary. On a national level receiving the status means that you are a nationally recognised healthy school, that is, as stated earlier, a school:

> ...that is successful in helping pupils to do their best and build on their achievements. It is committed to ongoing improvement and development. It promotes physical and emotional health by providing accessible and relevant information and equipping pupils with the skills and attitudes to make informed decisions about their health. A healthy school understands the importance in investing in health to assist in the process of raising levels of pupil achievement and improving standards. It also recognised the need to provide both a physical and social environment that is conductive to learning.

> (DfEE, 1999b, p2)

One school, on gaining the National Healthy School Standard accreditation, invited the healthy schools team to present the award. An award ceremony was set up and parents and the local community were invited to attend. A local sports star agreed to come and say a few words about the importance of the achievement (which helped with the advertising of the event). The ceremony involved local media and all who had worked in the school to achieve the award. As the issue that the school had worked on had been the creation of a safe playing area, the sports star, a pupil and a parent cut a red ribbon to signify the opening of the new safe play zone.

Step Nine: Celebrate

It is important that as a school you recognise and celebrate your achievements. This can be done in various ways: it may be that you hold a non-uniform day attributed to healthy school status or that you have a afternoon on healthy school type activities for pupils. Staff need also to have their achievements recognised, this can be done verbally by management in the school and/or local publicity on the newspaper.

Case-study

When a Year 5 Circle Time group completed their sessions the pupils felt that they wanted to share what they had learnt with the whole school. On the pupils' request a school assembly around Circle Time was run. The Year 5 class gave an interactive demonstration lesson involving the audience. All the pupils who had been involved in the initial Circle Time received a Circle Time certificate and then as a surprise to the Circle Time facilitators the pupils gave them thank you cards and chocolates for running the sessions. Not only did the assembly promote the value of Circle Time in the school, it also motivated more year groups and staff to be involved. The school now runs Circle Time with all its classes and has special award assemblies to issue certificates at the end of each half term.

Step Ten: Ongoing Reviews

It is essential that once the action plan has been devised that it is reviewed regularly. It will be the role of the task group to meet on a regular basis to update on what has been developed, what challenges there may have been and what has been completed. This information should not simply remain with the task group but also be fed back to the school community using the methods of communication outlined above.

Throughout this entire process it is essential to have your LEA involved and the Healthy School Co-ordinator or stand leader on emotional health and wellbeing from your area. Remember they will be the organisation issuing the National Healthy Schools Award so they will need to agree your action plan, be provided with evidence, remain updated about your progress and so forth. It is crucial you involve them right at the start of the process and keep them involved throughout.

Case-study

One school regularly ensures that time is allocated bi-annually for the school community to reflect on practice and developments around the Healthy Schools Standard which they achieved. This helps to ensure that the good practice the school established continues to be at the forefront of everyone's thinking and that the changes are sustained and integrated. It also helps evaluate practice on an ongoing basis so refinements can be made should they be required. For pupils this review takes place throughout Circle Time, which is used to explore each class's thoughts and feelings on the range of healthy school activities. For staff, workshops are conducted through a twilight session (in replace of a staff meeting); during this time staff are encouraged to reflect on good practice, what is going well and not so well, share ideas and brainstorm ideas for moving further forward. Parents are sent regular questionnaires to fill out regarding concerns, general feedback and impacts on children. All the contributions are collected bi-annually by the task group and reviewed; should any further action be required as a result of the feedback then the task group are able to ensure that it happens.

Healthy Schools Action Plan: An Example

School: Fictional Primary School
Year: 2004
Theme: Emotional Health and Wellbeing
Healthy Schools Co-ordinator: Mrs Wellbeing

How did you come to choose this theme?

Local need

Evidence collected from inter-agency/school meetings, local newspapers, and local research projects looking at a range of issues relating to young people in the area suggests that low self-esteem and a lack of awareness of personal safety is a barrier to making positive health choices and contributes to low educational achievement and social exclusion.

School need

Our whole-school audit, that included consultation with pupils, staff, parents, carers and other agencies within our community, showed a lack of knowledge of school policy and putting those policies into practice to be our weakest point. Staff concerns were raised during team meetings regarding the lack of consistency regarding discipline, recognition for achievements, response to bullying behaviour and in the delivery of Personal, Social, Health Education and Citizenship.

Aims

- to ensure the whole school is fulfilling their responsibility to developing effective and relevant PSHE and Citizenship that would promote pupils' spiritual, moral, social and cultural development and prepare all pupils for the opportunities, responsibilities and experiences of life

- to raise the confidence and capability of all staff to empower pupils, to raise their self-esteem and enable them to make positive life choices

- to increase and sustain partnership working with local agencies and young people's services

- to provide and promote healthier lifestyles for the whole school community.

Objectives

1. To set up and sustain a healthy schools task group to fulfil the schools aims

2. To design and deliver an inclusive emotional health and wellbeing programme for the whole school

3. To establish and support the roles required to develop and maintain the programme

4. To review and update school policies, development plans and plans of work to reflect the healthy school aims

5. To significantly raise the self-esteem and personal/academic achievement of pupils and celebrate those achievements

6. To monitor and evaluate staff personal and professional development and fulfil their emotional health and wellbeing needs

7. To proactively involve parents/carers in all aspects of school life

8. To encourage and sustain the involvement of outside agencies in all aspects of school life.

Objective 1

Activity: To set up and sustain a healthy schools task group to fulfil the schools aims (above).

Role: Head Teacher, Healthy School Scheme Co-ordinator

Time: Sept 2004

Method: The whole school community (including all staff, parents, carers, governors, external agencies and pupils) to be consulted on the creation of the task group, opportunities to become a member and be made aware of the task group members and roles.

Evidence to support: Contributors named in policy documents and prospectus. Minutes of task group and other focus groups recorded and available to whole school. Updates to be presented at assemblies, staff and governor meetings, open days and parent's evenings.

Objective 2

Activity: To design and deliver an inclusive emotional health and wellbeing programme for the whole school.

Role: Task Group

Time: Nov 2004

Method: Research to be carried out on all appropriate resources, training courses and staff experience and knowledge of emotional health and wellbeing issues, both curriculum and non-curriculum.

Evidence to support: Completed inclusive programme is published, distributed and delivered. Lessons are observed and recorded; resulting work is displayed in school album, prospectus and display areas (such as classrooms, hall, offices, reception, internal and external).

Objective 3

Activity: To establish and support the roles required to develop and maintain the programme.

Role: Task Group

Time: Dec 2004

Method: The whole school community (including all staff, parents, carers, governors, external agencies and pupils) to be consulted on the programme from draft to completion and made aware of the programme content, philosophy and process.

Role: Head Teacher, Senior Management Team, Governors

Time: Oct 2004

Method: Head Teacher, Senior Management and Governors to establish a firm commitment to the HSS Action Plan and participate in the Task Group, in regard to meetings, activity and consulting with the whole school community through their specific roles within the school.

Evidence to support: Endorsement of Task Groups terms of reference, job roles and time allocation to those roles. Reports from progress and activity at various HT, SMT and Governor meetings.

Objective 4

Activity: To review and update school policies, development plans and plans of work to reflect the healthy school aims.

Role: Task Group

Time: Dec 2004

Method: Drugs and SRE policy are revised to National Guidance Standards. There is a confidentiality policy, an updated Child Protection policy with procedures and a new bullying policy is completed.

Evidence to support: Up to date Drugs and SRE policy in line with National Guidance completed and available to whole school community.

Up to date bullying policy provided to all staff, pupils and sent home to all parents/carers.

Objective 5

Activity: To significantly raise the self-esteem and personal/ academic achievement of pupils and celebrate those achievements.

Role: Task Group, Head Teacher, Senior Management Team

Time: Sept 2004

Method: To creatively and consistently monitor and evaluate pupils' progress in relation to emotional health and wellbeing. Through recording behaviour, reported incidents and achievements.

Role: All Staff

Time: On-going

Method: Through the creation and delivery of pre and post questionnaires, behaviour improvement plans, classroom discipline plan, school's merits and awards system and incidents log book. The use of displays, photo albums and portfolios as visual expressions of work carried out and successes achieved.

Evidence to support: Evaluation report on the outcomes of the self-esteem questionnaires. A reduction in bullying behaviour, a reduction in disruptive behaviour, a reduction in absences from school. An increase in academic achievements and merits awarded.

Achievements, work and activities visually displayed around the whole school, including reception, offices, classrooms, hall, information boards as well as in the school newsletter.

Objective 6

Activity: To monitor and evaluate staff personal and professional development and fulfil their emotional health and wellbeing needs

Role: Head Teacher, Individual Staff

Time: Sept 2004, on-going

Method: To monitor and evaluate staff progress in relation to emotional health and wellbeing. To establish a clear induction process, staff audits and questionnaires, staff development plans, formal, structured and regular supervision. To include absence records, achievements, training needs and professional development.

Induction procedures revised through staff consultation, to construct individual staff development plans, to record, monitor and assess personal and professional progress. Staff training needs are consistently reviewed and skills base updated.

Evidence to support: A reduction in staff absence, a greater staff retention. All staff have ongoing development plans. Recognition of training and professional development through certificates displayed and acknowledged, alongside various successes and achievements throughout the school.

Objective 7

Activity: To proactively involve parents/carers in all aspects of school life.

Role: Task Group

Time: Sept 2004, on-going

Method: To monitor and evaluate parent's/carer's participation within the school. To actively involve parents/carers in all aspects of school life.

Using formal and informal methods of inviting parents/carers into consulting, participating and supporting school activities and celebrations. Including school trips, assemblies, classroom support, playtimes, parent's evening, special events, roles and responsibilities on task groups and working groups, governors meetings, and so on.

Evidence to support: Parents/carers are included within the displays celebrating success and achievements; parents/carers are present on task groups and working groups. Parents/carers have access to and are included on training courses and receive recognition for participation and effort.

Objective 8

Activity: To encourage and sustain the involvement of outside agencies in all aspects of school life

Role: Task Group, Head Teacher, Senior Management Team, All Staff

Time: Sept 2004

Method: Include outside agencies in the design and delivery of the inclusive emotional health programme, including resources, training, and consultancy and teaching aspects of the programme. School staff to participate in community network meetings and relevant events and projects to share good practice, increase knowledge base and skills for all staff.

Evidence to support: School staff (teaching and non-teaching staff) are included on community network groups; pupils are included in outside agencies, projects and programmes. Displays of work and successes are identified and celebrated within the school and within other community events.

Chapter Three

Preparing for an Emotional Health and Wellbeing Programme

Outlined in Chapter Four and Five are two eight session programmes, one for Key Stage 1 and one for Key Stage 2. The programmes can be delivered with pupils in a number of ways including whole class sessions or small group sessions. Whichever form you choose to apply to the programme its function and aims remain the same, that is, to develop the emotional health and wellbeing of pupils in the school. It is so often a misjudgement that schools are there to teach solely an academic curriculum; what we need to remember, however, is that many young people coming into the education system do not have the social or emotional skills that form the backbone of the learning process. If a child is not emotionally healthy or emotionally ready to learn they will not engage in the academic learning process as well as a child who is emotionally healthy. Thus by implementing a programme such as the one suggested in Chapter Four, alongside the academic curriculum, you are addressing the holistic needs of the child and helping them develop socially, emotionally and academically. Of course at the same time through the implementation of this programme you are showing progress towards developing as a healthy school under the theme of 'Emotional Health and Wellbeing, Including Bullying' and are on a sure path to achieving your NHSS Accreditation.

Programme Content

The following table briefly outlines the session content of the Key Stage 1 and Key Stage 2 emotional health and wellbeing programme in relation to the four statutory components of PSHE and Citizenship for primary schools. This table can be photocopied for staff to give them an overview of the whole programme in preparation for delivery of the individual sessions. The school could also use this table to plan clear links if you are considering amalgamating the current work that the school does under PSHE and Citizenship with this programme.

The four components of PSHE and Citizenship at Key Stage 1 and 2

1. Developing confidence and responsibility and making the most of their abilities

Key Stage 1	Key Stage 2
Session 1: This is Me	**Session 1: This is Me**
• To develop an awareness of one's self. • To reflect on one's own likes and dislikes. • To understand one's own strengths. • To recognise uniqueness and be proud of one's self.	• To enable pupils to express themselves in a positive way. • To help pupils become more aware of what is unique about them. • To understand one's own strengths and areas for improvement.
Session 2: Feelings	**Session 2: Feelings**
• To help pupils recognise feelings. • To help pupils to name feelings. • To help pupils start to identify how they feel.	• To enable pupils to express a range of different feelings. • To develop a feelings vocabulary. • To develop appropriate responses to others' feelings.

2. Preparing to play an active role as citizens

Key Stage 1	Key Stage 2
Session 3: Communication	**Session 3: Communication**
• To teach the skills of listening. • To encourage pupils to listen to adults. • To encourage pupils to listen to instructions. • To provide opportunity to practise the skills of listening.	• To explore the different methods of communication. • To provide opportunity to develop group discussion skills. • To practise listening and feedback skills.
Session 4: Choice	**Session 4: Choice**
• To help pupils recognise their ability to make choices. • To practise making decisions. • To encourage pupils to take part in discussions about matters relating to their life.	• To give pupils the opportunity to contribute to decisions. • To help pupils understand how their decisions affect others. • To help pupils recognise their ability to make choices.

3. Developing a healthy, safer lifestyle

Key Stage 1	Key Stage 2
Session 5: Personal safety	**Session 5: Personal safety**
• To explore the range of people who help keep pupils feeling safe. • To explore the feelings around safety. • To help children recognise the ways they can help themselves feel safe.	• To explore how we can stay safe when we may be in 'emotional' or 'physical' difficulty. • To introduce the concept of peer pressure. • To examine different ways of saying 'no'.

Key Stage 1	Key Stage 2
Session 6: Keeping others safe	**Session 6: Keeping others safe**
• To develop skills in communication and co-operation.	• To develop skills in communication, co-operation and working in groups.
• To explore ways of keeping others safe.	• To develop pupils recognition of when and how others may feel unsafe.
• To introduce the concept that there is no right without responsibility.	• To explore ways that pupils can help one another be and stay safe, specifically in the context of bullying.

4. Developing good relationships and respecting the differences between people

Key Stage 1	Key Stage 2
Session 7: Relationships	**Session 7: Relationships**
• To help individuals understand the importance of friends and friendship.	• To explore the skills involved in making and maintaining friends.
• To enhance social skills around friendships.	• To recognise other people's feelings when there are problems with friendships.
• To examine the skills involved in making friendship work.	• To think about the skills that pupils possess in relation to friendships.

Key Stage 1	Key Stage 2
Session 8: Difference	**Session 8: Difference**
• To explore the similarities and difference between pupils. • To help people celebrate each other's individual qualities.	• To celebrate difference and diversity. • To explore the ways that the group or class are similar and different. • To provide opportunity to reflect on one's personal qualities and differences. • To help pupils recognise and challenge stereotypes. • To explore pupils' attitudes to difference.

Programme Application

The school can choose to implement the programme in one of three ways, as outlined below, and the materials provided are flexible and can be used in each of the different settings. The programme has been written in the main for whole class groups, but replacement activities for small groups are suggested throughout the lesson plans so that the facilitator can make adaptations dependent on group size and dynamics where necessary.

1.   Whole-school Approach: The emotional health sessions can be applied via small group work to a given year group. Here everyone in the year group has the emotional health curriculum built into their timetable for a set amount of weeks.

2.   One-off Groups: The sessions can be used to raise self-esteem, build friendships and discuss current topics or to aid social development with a small group of children from a given year group.

3.   Class: The programme can be delivered with whole classes during PSHE slots or slots allocated to Citizenship. The programme can be delivered in its entirety as PSHE/Citizenship or simply to help build on the PSHE/Citizenship curriculum that is already established.

Setting up an Emotional Health and Wellbeing Programme with Small and One-off Groups

Should the school decide to set up small groups, rather than use the programme with classes, the following factors need to be taken into consideration by the group facilitator in order to ensure the success of small group work.

With any groups, large or small, there are a number of things that can affect effectiveness, cohesiveness and outcome. These include factors such as whether members are there by choice or not, why people have come to the group, what makes them want to come back every time, what people expect to achieve from the group, what individuals' expectations are, whether the group's expectations are the same and whether the group know one another or not. These aspects need to be addressed in Session One.

Other influencing factors include how many people are in the group, how long the group is to last, the frequency of meetings, and the make-up of the group, i.e. age, gender, religion, class and race, and the environment. The checklist below outlines good practice in setting up the emotional health programme to help ensure the most effective process and successful outcome.

The Room

It is important that the facilitator is allocated a room to undertake the sessions if they are not delivering it in their classroom. Using the library or hall creates difficulties and distractions. The room used should project a friendly and comfortable environment to create a safe place for the sessions to be undertaken. Ideally, the same room needs to be used on a weekly basis to provide consistency.

Frequency and Duration

The frequency and duration of sessions is governed by varying levels of concentration. The recommended time slot for primary aged pupils is 30 minutes. This may vary depending on the group size and dynamics of the group. Consistency in sessions is important and it is suggested they take place on a weekly basis. Sessions stretched over any length of time decrease the chances of pupils retaining the skills.

Seating Arrangements

It is ideal if the sessions take place in a circle. Chairs should be prearranged into a circle ready for the lesson. All barriers should be removed, desks put to the side of the room and enough space created to allow movement of pupils. The sessions have been developed so that pupils can remain seated in their classroom at their tables if this is more convenient for the class teacher or facilitator.

Using the technique of sitting in a circle creates a sense of unity, co-operation and equality; it ensures that:

- Everyone in the group, including the teacher, is equal – i.e. there is no 'controller'.
- Everyone can be seen and heard.
- People can make eye contact, which is an important aspect of speaking and listening.
- The group can work together to support one another.
- There are no physical barriers such as desks and chairs.
- Everyone is valued as an important member of the group.

It is important to create a relaxed, comfortable atmosphere for the group. It is best to start by letting pupils sit where they like in the circle; rather than being prescriptive and authoritative the facilitator can use games to get the group mixed up and split friendship groups (see below for a range of mixing games). It is important that the group facilitator sits in the circle with the pupils as an equal; this gives the pupils the message that the facilitator is not a controller, but an equal member of the group, which is particularly important in developing an atmosphere of trust between facilitators and children. It is also important that the facilitator is an active participant and joins in all the activities.

Mixing Games

Games are an excellent tool in allowing a legitimate reason to move. Have a bank of mixing games at hand, for example:

Change Seats

Aims: mixing game, legitimate movement and fun.

Resources: none.

What to do: Based on a theme (cars, desserts, fruit, countries) choose four categories (for cars it could be Mini, Escort, BMW, Ferrari; for desserts it could be cheesecake, trifle, ice cream, sticky toffee pudding). Going around the circle label pupils in turn based on your four categories. Explain to pupils that when you call out a category those who have been labelled as that category are to get up and change places. When you call out a phrase related to the categories (motorway madness for cars, dessert tray for cakes, fruit baskets for fruits, wide world for countries) they all get up and change places.

Zoom Zoom

Aims: mixing game, legitimate movement and fun.

Resources: none.

What to do: Sitting in the circle explain to pupils that when the facilitator says, 'zoom zoom' followed by the name of two pupils, those pupils are to change places as quickly as they can. Explain that zoom zoom will be used at random points and that they will need to listen carefully for it creeping in.

Change Places If...

Aims: changing places.

Resources: none.

What to do: Ask the pupils to change places if they have brown hair, if their birthday is in the summer, if they have a pet at home, if they like maths etc. Create a range of change places statements that can be used to mix the group when it is needed.

A variation of this game is to remove one chair from the circle and ask the person without a chair to stand in the centre of the circle and make a 'change places if' statement. When everyone changes places the person in the centre is to try and find a seat. The person left standing is to be the next to say a 'change places if...' statement.

Number Change

Aims: legitimate movement, mixing pupils, fun.

Resources: none.

What to do: Number each pupil in the circle as well as the facilitator. The facilitator removes their chair, stands in the centre of the circle and calls out two numbers. The pupils who are those numbers have to get up and change seats. The facilitator aims to steal one of the vacant chairs to leave one of the pupils without a seat. The pupil standing now shouts out two further numbers and again they change seats. Continue until the group is mixed.

Numbers

The number of pupils engaged in the emotional health programme at any one time can vary considerably, depending on the application chosen. For small group work the ideal size is about eight. Small groups help personalise individuals in the group and increase their sense of belonging and value to the group. Small groups with large numbers are more difficult to manage and very large groups can be time consuming; doing a round, for example, can involve a lot of waiting and very small groups do not provide enough peer support for pupils. Activities for large groups need to be short and pupils need to be encouraged to keep answers brief.

Pupils

If there are targeted pupils in the group for behavioural needs, numbers should be kept to a minimum so that negative and/or disruptive behaviours are challenged and positive role models are prevalent to promote change. In cases such as these the suggestion is two targeted pupils to six role model pupils. Pupils with behavioural difficulties often respond well to the emotional health and wellbeing environment, they may feel more in control, have more individualised and positive attention and there are vast opportunities to raise self-esteem and help pupils feel good about themselves. Pupils with emotional problems also benefit from this curriculum, the range of techniques applied to deliver the programme ensure shy or withdrawn pupils are included. The emotional health and wellbeing (including bullying) curriculum can help develop confidence and a sense of self.

If pupils in the group have learning difficulties there may be a need to differentiate the work for them. This means that worksheets may need to be adapted, learning styles varied and more in depth explanations given. However, the emotional health and wellbeing curriculum is more active and oral than reading and writing, which means that pupils with learning difficulties will perhaps suffer fewer disadvantages in the learning styles than they may in the classroom. Pupils with other special educational needs such as visually impaired or hearing impaired pupils can also be included into emotional health and wellbeing groups, there is support in the curriculum from the teacher as well as peers, and the work is of a co-operative, helping and caring nature. Be sure to know the make-up of your group to account for their needs and have the appropriate resources.

The Role of the Group Facilitator

The facilitator is the key to the success of the course. A teacher, a school based mentor or an external agency, for example, an educational social worker, can adopt the role of the facilitator. The role that the facilitator will play is very diverse; it involves organising sessions, times and venues, preparing work and resources, facilitating sessions and structuring the learning experience and responding to emotional issues. The facilitator will be seen as a model for personal and social behaviours as well as attitudes, morals and values. Korfkamp (1998) outlines the 'needs' in relation to the role of a group facilitator:

The group facilitator needs to:

- make each pupil feel important and valued

- make sure that each pupil is listened to and heard

- encourage participation

- be aware of what is going on in different groups

- keep pupils on task by clarifying instructions

- encourage positive feedback

- pay attention to individual pupils when necessary

- allow pupils to have the same opportunities.

The facilitator needs to participate actively in the process. The input will be most effective when it is seen by the children as a guide, not a judge, pointing out right or wrong, good or bad (White, 1999).

Rules

In all aspects of society we have rules. An analogy I often use with young people is through posing the question, 'What would happen on a football pitch if there were no rules?' or, 'If we didn't have any laws what might happen?' After this pupils often agree that where people come together to work, to play or to socialise there are a set of rules involved. Sometimes these rules are written down, at other times these rules are 'unwritten', that is, we behave or act in a certain ways that we believe, based on our culture or value system, are most appropriate for the situation we are in and for the role we are taking.

The course is flexible but, as with all successful structures, there needs to be some consensus of what is acceptable behaviour. Rules are important as they provide a framework within which relationships can develop and grow in a positive way (Curry and Bromfield, 1998).

It is important that the group has ownership over their rules. To do this pupils in a group can free-think and record ideas for rules onto a large piece of paper. They can negotiate priorities and select ones they wish to operate within the group. This way they will own the rules and therefore be much more likely to adhere to them. It also takes the pressure off the leader from being the law-enforcing authority.

Some rules that groups have evolved are:

- listen to one another
- talk one at a time
- respect the ideas and values of others
- keep personal comments positive
- opportunity to pass
- confidentiality.

Once the rules have been decided they can be displayed on the wall for the remainder of the group time together.

To ensure that pupils follow their rules, it is important to be clear to the pupils that they are the ones to decide when someone is breaking a rule and what needs to happen as a result. A pupil, for example, could be asked to leave the circle or class until they feel they can return and follow the rule. Whatever consequence is imposed, be sure that it is a consensus among the group as to whether an individual deserves it; this way the facilitator is not solely responsible for what happens in the group.

Individuals making up the group can reflect on one another's behaviour based on the rules that they have decided to operate. This again places ownership on the rules and incrcascs the likelihood of adhering to them. Be sure that pupils, as well as the facilitator, also openly acknowledge and praise one another for following the rules. Remember, what we pay attention to is what we get more of.

Two important aspects to elaborate on with pupils are that of confidentiality and 'passing'.

Confidentiality

The contract between pupils needs to include one of confidentiality. It is the role of the facilitator to ensure that pupils understand the concept of confidentiality and apply it to the group situation. It can be an agreement between pupils that they will not discuss what other pupils have talked about with anybody outside the group. This helps develop a climate of trust, setting an ethos where pupils feel able to express themselves and 'take risks'.

It is important to explore confidentiality in the early stages of meeting the group with whom you will be working and to establish clear boundaries. A 'verbal contract' needs to be made which all pupils and the facilitator can refer back to. The contract needs to state what both the pupils and the facilitator are aiming for – what can be expected as well as what cannot be provided.

In conjunction with child protection law, limits to what can be kept confidential will occur if someone discloses they have been physically injured or abused, this includes:

- physical abuse
- emotional abuse
- sexual abuse
- neglect.

Confidentiality of the facilitator may need to be broken if someone is experiencing severe emotional distress, if there are any concerns about the person's safety or welfare, or if the facilitator has any doubts about their ability to assist the pupil.

The pass rule

It is important that pupils who engage in the emotional health programme do not feel pressurised or uncomfortable participating. The range of techniques allow for a variety of ways to engage pupils, so those who may not wish to speak in front of a large group have the opportunity to undertake work in pairs, on worksheets or in small groups. It may be that at points in the emotional health and wellbeing curriculum programme a pupil does not wish to participate, in this situation the pupil has the right to pass. At the end of the activity it is important to return to the pupil and allow them the opportunity to answer, contribute or comment if they wish to; they still have the opportunity to pass should they wish.

Encouraging Active Listening

The group work sessions also improve the speaking and listening process. Many of the activities, teaching methods and games involve the skill of active listening, a skill that involves offering our full attention to another. Curry and Bromfield (1998) identify ten components of active listening:

1. Having eye contact with the person who is talking.

2. Giving full attention.

3. Sitting quietly without distracting the person who is talking.

4. Focusing on the speaker's needs.

5. Showing that you understand.

6. Letting the speaker express feelings without interruption or putdown.

7. Asking no questions.

8. Making no comments of your own.

9. Showing appropriate non-verbal behaviour.

10. Communicating acceptance no matter what the speaker is saying.

It is important that the facilitator also actively listens to group members. Based on what is disclosed or discussed, what values or attitudes emerge and what feelings are expressed it is not the role of the facilitator to give advice, make comments or judgements, provide sympathy or solutions, agree, disagree, argue, praise or blame.

The role of the facilitator is to model behaviour: to listen and accept individuals and to take a neutral role. Active listening is important to provide an atmosphere of co-operation, trust, acceptance and mutual regard.

It is important that the facilitator encourages pupils in the group to actively listen to one another. This can be done through establishing rules, playing listening games, using a talking object and adopting appropriate techniques that encourage listening.

Managing Emotions

Within the group situation pupils may experience a range of both positive and negative emotions. It is important that the facilitator is able to deal with pupils' emotions. As noted earlier sometimes feelings are obvious and are apparent in an individual's verbal or non-verbal behaviour. As a facilitator, being able to read the feelings of the individuals in the group can be an important contributor to its success as a whole as well as for individuals within in it. According to White (1999) a facilitator of small group work needs to have 'personal warmth' demonstrated by a good vocabulary of feelings and sensitivity to emotional needs; the facilitator also needs to be comfortable in dealing with emotional issues.

Follow-ups

It is important that if information is disclosed that either falls within the realms of child protection, if the pupil appears to be experiencing severe emotional distress, or if there are any concerns about the person's safety or welfare, that the facilitator conducts a follow-up session with the pupil. The follow-up session may be undertaken with the facilitator or the facilitator accompanied by a person who is more experienced in handing such situations. If a pupil makes a disclosure within a group situation it is appropriate to acknowledge it by saying something along the lines of, 'That seems like something you can talk to me about when the group has finished, could you stay and talk to me at the end.'

Pupils with emotional problems benefit immensely from engaging in group work of this nature as it helps enhance self-esteem and confidence. Thus the facilitator needs to ensure that a positive ethos develops within the group and that there are ample opportunities for affirmation, positive self-review and praise, and that a range of activities is included to promote this.

Managing Behaviour

Within group situations challenging behaviours may arise. It is important that pupils with behaviour problems are not simply excluded as much of the time this type of support helps challenge and change behaviour patterns. Increasing the self-esteem of pupils so they feel better about themselves can have a huge influence on behaviour. To help avoid disruptive behaviour in the group and address them if they arise look at the checklist below that describes a number of strategies and forward planning principles that can be of use to the facilitator.

Gaining quiet

The programme involves playing games and games, as well as groups in general, can become very noisy. So for these reasons it is important for the facilitator and the participants to agree a signal that indicates the need for quiet. This can be a clap of the hands, the blow of a whistle or a bang on the wall. Inform the pupils that any time they hear this signal they need to return to their seats and stop talking. If the group finds this difficult make it a fun exercise i.e. the first person gets a prize and the last person has to play a simple (but fun) forfeit.

Set clear rules and expectations

Ensure that a set of group rules has been devised, that they are clear, that pupils understand them and that they are displayed. Try and phrase the rules positively stating the behaviour that you want. For example, rather than the rule, 'Don't all talk at once' state the rule as, 'One person to talk at a time; raise your hand to signal to talk'. Make sure any new rules that are introduced into the group i.e. rules for a game that is to be played, are given clearly and concisely. Use the rules to praise pupils when they are good and offer consequences as a choice. Ensure that when dealing with a disruptive situation you label the act and not the child (for example, 'I like you but I don't like it when you choose to interrupt other people', rather than, 'You are a rude person').

Opportunities for praise

Catch the pupils being good. Even difficult pupils are good sometimes - be sure to praise them if they are doing the right things. Most people watch for disruptive behaviour. Use at least three times as many praise statements as negative ones. Try to start and finish every session with a positive. Start every session with a clean slate - give everyone a chance to choose positive consequences first.

Forward planning

Don't arrive for the lesson at the same time as the pupils; you will need to forward plan. Make sure the room is ready, materials are prepared, their work is displayed on the wall and the rules are up and so forth. Ensure that you know the lesson plan, make sure that the activities in the lesson plan fit the group that you are working with and keep the lesson clear, interesting and moving at a brisk pace.

Use incentives

The uses of games throughout the curriculum are excellent incentives for pupils. Games can be used as an incentive for finishing an activity. Other incentives may be personalised to the individuals in the group.

Have a sense of humour

Using your own sense of humour, sharing yourself with the pupils and being an active part of the group will help bridge a relationship between the facilitator and the pupils. The effect of this on pupils' behaviour is enormous.

Look for causes of problems

Analyse any problems after the session. It is important to reflect by asking yourself why the problem occurred and what the source of the problem may be; sometimes there is a simple solution that can be acted on. It may be that a follow-up session is needed with a pupil or pupils who are causing particular difficulties and they can be set an individual target within the group to help them stay focused and on task.

Promote pupil responsibility

Prepare the rules as a group, allow pupils to decide on consequences (positive and negative), allow pupils to choose a game, allow pupils to contribute, give pupils different responsibilities, use peer tutoring, offer choices and so on. Ensure pupils are in control over their participation, that is, allow them to pass. Pupil responsibility is empowering and allows pupils to develop their own learning environment.

Facilitator behaviour

Ensure you are a role model for the pupils: be confident in your approach, show good non-verbal communication, use positive and clear language, have a positive belief and attitude and build relationships with pupils. The behaviour of the facilitator, the language used and the choices made have a profound effect on the pupils and the success of the group.

Use games

Games are an excellent tool: if you feel that the group needs a legitimate reason to move, needs a boost of energy, needs to laugh or inappropriate pairings/groups need to be split up, then play a game. Have a bank of games in reserve that you can call on.

Chinese Fingers

Aims: concentration, fun.

Resources: none.

What to do: Sitting in the circle pupils face the back of the person sitting on their left. A pupil is chosen to start and they draw a simple shape or a number on the back of the person they are looking at. This pupil then copies the shape or number they think was drawn onto their back onto the back of the pupil they are facing. This continues around the circle until it reaches the last person in the circle who states the number or shape they believe was drawn on their back.

Copy the Leader

Aims: concentration.

Resources: none.

What to do: In the circle a leader is chosen who starts a simple movement. All pupils are to copy the movement. Once all pupils have got the movement the leader adds another movement. This continues until the movements are too complex to remember. A variation on this is that prior to the leader being chosen one or two pupils are sent out of the room. When the leader has been decided they re-enter and their task is to guess which pupil is leading the group.

Balloons

Aims: legitimate movement, fun, energiser.

Resources: balloons.

What to do: You will need three to four blown up balloons for a small group and six to eight for a large group. The facilitator explains that the object of the game is to keep the balloons in the air at all times. Each person however must remain in their space in front of their chair, they can reach inwards, outwards or sideways to prevent the balloon from touching the floor.

Touch Down

Aims: legitimate movement, concentration, balance and fun.

Resources: none.

What to do: Ask pupils to form pairs. The facilitator calls out a number. The pupils' task is to have the equivalent number of points (feet, elbows, hands, knees) touching the floor. The last person to touch down with the right number of points is out; continue until there is a winner. Pupils can form groups of three, four of five to make the task more difficult.

Simon Says

Aims: communication, concentration.

Resources: none.

What to do: The facilitator gives a range of instructions to follow, for example, put your hands on your head, touch your left knee, raise your right arm, point to the door, touch your nose. When the instruction is given with the sentence, 'Simon says…' in front of it pupils need to follow the direction; if it does not start with this then pupils need to ignore the instruction. When a pupil follows an instruction that didn't start with 'Simon says' they are out. Continue until you have a winner.

Ignore minor disruptions

Rather than focus on minor disruptions, direct your attention onto a pupil who is displaying the behaviour that you want to achieve in the group and make a clear positive statement. For example, if a pupil is fidgeting and you need them to be still turn your attention to a given pupil, use their name and say, 'Thank you … you are sitting very still, that is what I need for this activity.' By doing this you are not giving negative attention to a specific pupil, you are being clear about your expectations and you are catching pupils being good. Remember that what you pay attention to is what you get more of.

Keeping time

It is a good idea to set time frames for pupils when there are activities to do so that they are aware of exactly how long they have to complete an activity. It is useful to give a verbal reminder of the remaining time frame for activities: saying ten minutes remaining, five minutes remaining, two minutes remaining and one minute remaining will help the children stay focused and on task during long activities. It may also be useful to tell the pupils the time they need to finish by, for example, 'You have five minutes to do this; you will need to finish by 3 o'clock', and then give the one-minute warning, 'You have one minute to finish what you are doing' at the end. Sometimes a ten second count-down to wrap up the closure of the activity can encourage pupils to put their pens down and refocus. An alternative idea is for the facilitator to have a signal for children to stop and focus. The signal maybe a clap, whistle, bell or sound of a musical instrument.

Starting and ending activities

As any good book or film demonstrates there needs to be a strong and interesting beginning and an ending. A good starting activity allows pupils to become involved and initiates interest and motivation from the onset, it 'buys' them into the activity or session, that is, they are stimulated and keen to engage in the rest of the session. When working with pupils it is essential to ensure that starting and ending activities are positive. A positive start sets the climate and a positive end leaves the children feeling good. The starting and ending activities used in the programme involve sentence completions and games. It is advisable to write the sentence completions onto the board or flip-chart for children so that they can clearly read and complete the sentence.

Using the Programme to Gain the National Healthy Schools Standard

Providing Evidence

To gain the NHSS you will need to supply your local healthy school team with evidence that you have met the objectives laid out in your action plan. Providing evidence can be done via a range of techniques including photographs, newsletter, evaluations and so on. Two methods of providing evidence are outlined below; these particular methods are good as they also help enforce the theme throughout the whole school and ensure that pupils, staff, parents and carers start to adopt the philosophy of becoming an emotionally healthy school.

Displaying work

By implementing the programme in Chapter Four the school will undoubtedly have an influence on the emotional health and wellbeing of the young people involved. One method of ensuring that effects are long lasting, and the theme of emotional health is embraced at all times around the school, is to use the work that is created during the session times in and around the school. The emotional health standard is about embracing a way of working that creates a safe and positive ethos in the school; by displaying pupils' work, reinforcing the themes of the session and putting posters up around the school, based on what has taken place in the lessons, are ways of achieving this. Displaying work is an integral part of the emotional health curriculum and will help you achieve your healthy schools status.

Photographs

With all the extra effort from the whole school community it is essential to capture the growth, fun and learning that develops as the activities and processes are applied throughout the school. It is part of the accreditation process to provide evidence of activity and growth as well as celebrating and recognising individual, group, class and whole-school achievement. Photographs create a visual sense of ownership, pride and belonging as well as being a great method to reinforce the principles and aspirations of the whole school.

Chapter Four

Emotional Health and Wellbeing Sessions for Key Stage 1 Pupils

Key Stage 1 Programme Delivery

The emotional health and wellbeing programme for Key Stage 1 comprises eight sessions. Each session lasts roughly thirty minutes and can be delivered to small groups or class groups. Where necessary adaptations to activities for varying group sizes are provided. Additional sessions to evolve the programme or extra activities to extend the sessions can be delivered if the school wishes to add to the package provided. Good practice on preparing to deliver the programme is outlined at the start of Chapter Two and needs to be read by the facilitator prior to delivery.

The lesson plans take the facilitator step-by-step clearly through each session. The aims of each session are stated, lesson plans are provided and all the resources that are required are included at the end of each session (these can be photocopied or printed from the CD-ROM included with this book). The sessions are highly interactive and are based on visual, auditory and kinaesthetic (VAK) learning and apply a range of facilitation techniques.

The following is a brief account of the curriculum agenda:

Session One: This is Me

This session is about exploring the concept of self, to enable pupils to reflect on those traits and qualities that make them who they are and encourage them to feel proud of their uniqueness and identity.

Session Two: Feelings

The focus of Session Two is identifying and recognising both emotional and physical everyday feelings, exploring those feelings and developing the confidence to share feelings with others.

Session Three: Communication

This session continues to build on basic life skills with the teaching of listening skills. Through following instructions, participating in groups and paired discussions and developing respect for others' ideas, thoughts and feelings.

Session Four: Choices

This session builds on pupils' listening and discussion skills through exploring behaviour choices, recognising and developing their ability to respond effectively to people and circumstances and make safe decisions for the benefit of themselves and others.

Session Five: Personal Safety

In this session pupils are provided with the opportunity to explore the range of people who help keep pupils feeling safe in and out of school. Safety feelings are explored and children start to examine ways they can keep themselves safe physically and emotionally.

Session Six: Keeping Others Safe

The aim of this session is to develop skills in communication and co-operation, explore ways of keeping others safe and introduce the concept that there is no 'right' without responsibility.

Session Seven: Relationships

The theme of this session is to enable pupils to develop an understanding of the importance of making friends and keeping friends. It aims to enhance social skills within this area as well as develop friendship maintenance skills.

Session Eight: Difference

The purpose of this session is to explore the similarities and differences between pupils as a way of looking at difference and diversity. The session also helps people celebrate each other's individual qualities.

Session One: This is Me

Aims

- to develop an awareness of one's self
- to reflect on one's own likes and dislikes
- to understand one's own strengths
- to recognise uniqueness and be proud of who we are.

Resources: For Classes

- overhead projector
- white card, A3, one per pupil
- old magazines
- coloured crayons and pencils
- pens and pencils
- scissors
- glue sticks
- skin colour crayons
- stool.

Resources: For Small Groups

- white paper, A4, one per pupil
- magazines cut-outs of children's hobbies
- pencils
- glue sticks.

Starting Activity: For Classes and Small Groups

Ask each child in the class or small group to complete the following round:

- Today my favourite colour is...

(For large classes ask each table to tell each other their answer and for small groups allow each pupil in the circle to complete the sentence in turn.)

Main Activity: For Classes

Your task it to get a silhouette of each child. Set up an overhead projector, projecting onto a piece of A3 white card. Place a stool in front for the child to sit on sideways this will cast their profile onto the piece of card; draw around each child in turn (you may want to do this prior to the session to save time). Once children have a silhouette of themselves ask them to:

- write their name and age on their work
- colour in the picture of themselves (hair, skin and eye colour) – use a skin coloured crayon set if you have one
- cut out pictures from magazines of things that they like doing and glue them on to their picture
- write the sentence, 'The best thing about being me is…' on their work and ask them to complete the sentence.

You will need to put magazines, scissors, glue sticks and colouring crayons on each table. The pictures can be used for a display in the classroom to celebrate the diversity of the class members and remind pupils of, 'things they like and what they are good at'.

Main Activity: For Small Groups

In the centre of the circle place lots of pictures of hobbies previously cut out from magazines; the pictures should consist of a range of things that represent hobbies, for example, playing on swings, walking, bike riding, cooking with parents, Play Station (you will need to have duplicates of pictures).

Ask each pupil in turn to go to the centre of the circle and pick out two pictures that they think reflect what they like doing. Once they have chosen the picture they are to say to the group, 'Two things I like doing are…' and hold up the pictures. Once everyone has collected their pictures, provide each person in the group with a piece of blank paper and ask each pupil to write their name on the top. Using glue help them stick their pictures to the paper.

Collect in the pupils' sheets and explain to the group that they are now going to play a game that involves each pupil leaving the room in turn and friends in the group helping the facilitator to write things that they are good at on to their poster. Ask one child at a time to leave the room; the remainder in the circle are to say two things that they like about the person who has left the room while the facilitator writes these on the poster of the relevant child. Ask the pupil to re-enter the room and tell them they will find out what has been said about them once everyone has had their turn. Once you have completed this activity for all pupils, return posters to their owners.

Ending Activity: For Classes

Ask the children to hold up their picture and complete the following sentence:

'This is me, I am proud that…'

Ending Activity: For Small Groups

Ask the pupils to hold up their poster in turn and as a group read out what it says on each poster, using the following words:

'This is (name of pupil) s/he likes (state what is in the two pictures). Two things s/he is good at are (state the two statements made).'

Session Two: Feelings

Aims

- to help pupils recognise feelings
- to help pupils to name feelings
- to help pupils start to identify how they feel.

Resources

- pack of Feelings Cards
- Feelings Faces worksheet – one per pupil.

Starting Activity: For Classes and Small Groups

Ask each child in the class to complete the following round:

- Today I feel…

Main Activity: For Classes and Small Groups

(Prior to this activity it is important that the teacher or group facilitator sorts out the cards based on the ability level of the pupils.)

Move the tables away and ask the pupils to sit in a circle on their chairs. Ask for a pupil to start. From the pack of Feelings Cards show the pupil the word on the card and whisper to them what it says. The pupil needs to act the feeling to the group or show it in their facial expression. The task of the group is to guess the feeling. Work your way through the pile of Feelings Cards.

Provide the pupils with the Feeling Faces handout. Ask them to work individually to complete the worksheet. The pictures can be used for a display to help provide pupils with a feeling vocabulary.

When the pupils have finished their pictures ask them to return to the group and in turn stand up and hold up their picture for the rest of the group to see.

Ending Activity: For Classes and Small Groups

Ask the children in the class to think of a feeling that starts with the same letter or initial sound of their name and then introduce themselves one at a time saying the feeling first followed by their name. For example, 'I am Cheerful Charlie.'

Feelings Cards

Photocopy, or print from the CD-ROM, these feelings on to card and cut them into individual word cards.

Friendly	Lonely	Sad
Interested	Worried	Surprised
Hurt	Cheerful	Angry
Mad	Sleepy	Threatened
Lazy	Ashamed	Proud
Silly	Scared	Embarrassed
Shocked	Upset	Bored
Nervous	Calm	Frustrated
Confused	Confident	Excited
Shy	Disappointed	Jealous
Lively	Safe	Pleased
Unsafe	Hot	Warm
Cold	Frozen	

Feelings Faces

How do these people feel?

What do you do for fun?

_____

_____

How do you feel when
you're having fun?

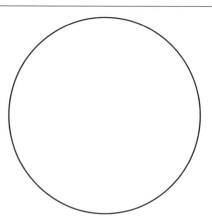

Session Three: Communication

Aims

- to teach the skills of listening
- to encourage pupils to listen to adults
- to encourage pupils to listen to instructions
- to provide opportunity to practise the skills of listening.

Resources

- Listening Circles - 'Stop' and 'Go' signs – one set (coloured red and green)
- Listening Skills handout – one per pupil.

Starting Activity: For Classes and Small Groups

As a class/group sing a familiar nursery rhyme or song. Explain to the pupils that when you hold up the red circle they are to stop singing and be silent and when you hold up the green circle they can start to sing again. During the nursery rhyme or song aim to stop and start the pupils three to four times.

Main Activity: For Classes and Small Groups

Play the game Simon Says: explain to the pupils that when an instruction is given that starts with the words 'Simon says' then they are to follow that instruction. Have pupils practise this using the following statements:

Simon says put your hands on your head.

Simon says touch your toes.

Simon says point to a window.

Now explain to the pupils that when you give an instruction that does not start with 'Simon says' they are not to follow it. Have a practice.

Simon says touch your nose.	Follow instruction – pupils touch nose.
Simon says fold your arms.	Follow instruction – pupils fold arms.
Jump up and down.	Do not follow instruction – pupils stay still.
Simon says turn around.	Follow instruction – pupils turn around.
Touch your knees.	Do not follow instruction – pupils stay still.

The game is played with pupils standing up. Each time a pupil follows an instruction that does not start with 'Simon says' they are to sit out. The winner is the last pupil left standing.

As pupils get better at the game the facilitator will need to speed up the rate at which they give instructions.

Activity Two: For Classes and Small Groups

Hand out the worksheet titled 'Listening Skills'. On the board or a flip-chart write down the same three sentences that are on the worksheet, leaving a gap under each to record pupil ideas. As a group ask pupils to give ideas about:

- how you can tell if someone is listening
- why we need to listen
- things pupils can do to help them listen better.

Make sure you write the answers clearly on the flip-chart or board. When you have finished ask the pupils as a group to read together all the ideas that are written up, and then ask each pupil individually to copy down their favourite idea onto the worksheet. You will need to wander round the class or group to help them.

Ending Activity: For Classes and Small Groups

Ask each child in the class to complete the following round:

- I can be a better listener by…

Listening Circles

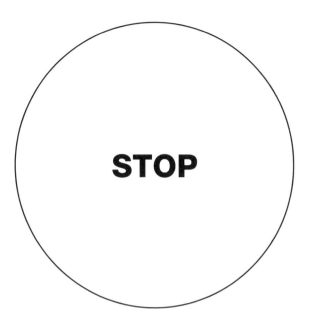

STOP

GO

Listening Skills

You can tell if someone is not listening because...

We need to listen because...

I can listen better by...

Session Four: Choices

Aims

- to help pupils recognise their ability to make choices
- to practise making decisions
- to encourage pupils to take part in discussions about matters relating to their life.

Resources

- Choice Cards – one card per pupil
- storybook of your choice.

Starting Activity: For Classes and Small Groups

Hand out a Choice Card to every child from the selection provided. Ask each pupil to make a choice about which item on the card he/she would prefer. Once everyone has made their choice allow everyone to give feedback in turn using the following sentence completion:

'I had to choose between… and…, what I chose was…'

(You may need to write this sentence on the chalkboard.)

Main Activity: For Classes and Small Groups

Choose one of the children's favourite storybooks to read, for example, *Little Red Riding Hood*, *Goldilocks* or *Snow White*.

At certain points in the text when a character is about to make a decision on something (i.e. taking an apple from the basket – Little Red Riding Hood; going into the house – Goldilocks; making the tea for the Dwarfs – Snow White) stop reading and ask the pupils what choices are available to the character. Work with the pupils to come up with a range of choices that the character has. Continue reading. Stop the text at least five times during the story to do this.

Resource: *Try Again Little Red Riding Hood: A New Look at an Old Story* by Gorden, S. and Litt, S. (1999). Essence Publications: Australia. This is an ideal resource for this exercise, it tells the story of Red Riding Hood stopping at key points and providing the reader with a series of prompts to ask pupils about feelings and choices of the characters. It also gets the children to come up with different endings to the book and look at the effects and consequences of the different decisions that are made throughout.

Ending Activity: For Classes and Small Groups

Ask each child in the class to complete the following round:

- One thing I choose about my behaviour at school is…

Choice Cards

Photocopy, or print from the CD-ROM, this page onto card and cut out each pair of choices to give you a set of Choice Cards.

Eat cereal for breakfast	Eat toast for breakfast
Have a bath before bed	Have a shower before bed
Wear the red top to the party	Wear the blue top to the party
Read when you come in from school	Watch TV when you come in from school
Talk to a friend	Go to the library
Play with the skipping rope	Play with the ball
Play running games	Play on the climbing frame
Play tick	Play board games
Have a drink of milk	Have a fizzy drink
Eat an apple	Eat an orange
Eat crisps for break	Eat chocolate for break
Have strawberry ice cream	Have chocolate ice cream

Go swimming on Saturday	Go for a bike ride on Saturday
Eat chips for tea	Have potatoes for tea
Paint your bedroom yellow	Paint your bedroom blue
Play snakes and ladder	Play card games
Do maths	Do English
Do your homework when you get in from school	Play with your friends when you get in from school
Listen to the teacher	Talk while the teacher is talking
Run down the corridor to assembly	Walk down the corridor to assembly
Line up quietly for dinner	Push in the dinner queue
Put you hand up to answer a question	Shout out the answer to a question
Have extra time on the carpet	Have extra time in the playground
Visit a zoo	Visit a museum
Visit a farm	Visit a castle
Play on the swings	Play on the side
Colour in a picture	Paint a picture
Play with Plasticene	Play with Lego

Have a boiled egg for breakfast	Have scrambled egg for breakfast
Watch a film	Help tidy up the house
Watch a cartoon on TV	Read a comic book
Go to the cinema to see a film	Have a new video game to play
Play indoors	Play outdoors
Put your toys away	Make your bed
Have a pet cat	Have a pet dog

Session Five: Personal Safety

Aims

- to explore the range of people who help keep pupils feeling safe
- to explore the feelings around safety
- to help children recognise the ways they can help themselves feel safe.

Resources For Classes

- worksheet Staying Safe at School – one per pupil
- one set of Sentence Completion Cards
- badges – one per pupil
- flip-chart and pen (optional)
- double sided tape (optional)
- one set of Prompt Cards
- support of a classroom assistant.

Resources For Small Groups

- white A4 paper – one piece per pupil
- pencils
- coloured crayons and pencils
- badges – one per pupil
- flip-chart and pen
- double sided tape (optional)
- one set of Prompt Cards.

Starting Activity: For Classes

Ask pupils to think about their safety at school, from when they leave the house in the morning to come to school to when they go home after school, and all the time they are in school.

Hand out to each pupil a Staying Safe at School worksheet and ask pupils to draw four people who keep them safe at school or on their way to and from school, and write the role this person plays underneath.

Examples that pupils can use are:

- lunch-time supervisors
- best friends
- teachers
- lollypop man/woman
- pupils
- school nurse
- bus driver.

Ask the pupils to give feedback about one of the people they have drawn.

Starting Activity: For Small Groups

Ask pupils to think about their safety at school, from when they leave the house in the morning to come to school to when the go home after school and all the time they are in school.

Ask each pupil in turn to finish the following sentence:

'Someone who helps keep me safe is...'

As the pupils come up with ideas record them clearly onto a flip-chart.

Main Activity: For Classes

For this activity you will need to split the class into two, with the classroom assistant working with one group and the class teacher with another.

This activity will need to take place with pupils sitting in a circle or round a table together. Going around the circle one pupil at a time ask each pupil to complete the following sentences in turn. Pass around the Sentence Completion Card to help pupils remember the prompt:

- A place I feel safe is...
- When I am safe I feel...
- I keep myself safe by...

Now as a group discuss what things we can ask for help with to help us feel safe:

- in the classroom
- on the playground
- on the way to and from school.

You may want to record the ideas as pupils come up with them onto a flip-chart.

Main Activity: For Small Groups

Ask all the pupils to lie on the floor with their eyes closed. Explain to them that you are going to ask them to think about some questions but they do not have to give you an answer, just think about it to themselves. Ask the pupils to:

- think of a place where they are safe and picture this place in their mind
- think about the colours that are in their safe place
- think about the smells that are in their safe place
- think about the noises that are in their safe place
- think about the people who are with them in their safe place
- take an imaginary walk around their safe place and think about how they feel when they are there.

Then ask pupils to slowly open their eyes and sit back on their chairs.

Provide each pupil with something to lean on and a piece on A4 white paper, put coloured crayons and pencils in the centre of the circle. Ask pupils to spend five minutes drawing their safe place. If time allows ask each pupil in turn to hold up their picture and complete the following sentence:

'A place I feel safe is…'

Activity Two: For Classes and Small Groups

Now as a group, using the Prompt Cards, discuss what things we can ask for help with to help us feel safe:

- in the classroom
- on the playground
- on the way to and from school.

You may want to record the ideas as pupils come up with them onto a flip-chart or chalkboard.

Optional Game: For Classes and Small Groups

Play a game of Touch Down. Ask pupils to form pairs. The facilitator calls out a number. The pupil's task is to have the equivalent number of points (feet, elbows, hands, knees) touching the floor. The last pair to touch down with the right number of points is out; continue until there is a winner. Pupils can form groups of three, four or five to make the task more difficult.

Explain to pupils that they need to keep themselves safe, as well as their partner, while playing this game.

Ending Activity: For Classes and Small Groups

Provide every pupil with an I Can Keep Myself Safe badge and ask him or her to colour in the smiley face in a colour of his or her choice. Each pupil can keep their badge. You may wish to give each child a piece of double sided sticky tape so they can stick it to themselves.

Staying Safe at School

Draw four people who keep you safe at school and write underneath what their role is.

This person keeps me safe	This person keeps me safe
This person is	This person is
This person keeps me safe	This person keeps me safe
This person is	This person is

I Can Keep Myself Safe Badge

Photocopy, or print from the CD-ROM, onto card and cut out (one per pupil).

Sentence Completion Cards

Photocopy, or print from the CD-ROM, one set.

A place I feel safe is…

When I am safe I feel…

I keep myself safe by…

Prompt Cards

Photocopy, or print from the CD-ROM, one set.

What things can we ask for help with in the classroom to help us feel safe?

What things can we ask for help with on the playground to help us feel safe?

What things can we ask for help with on the way to and from school to help us feel safe?

Session Six: Keeping Others Safe

Aims

- to develop skills in communication and co-operation
- to explore ways of keeping others safe
- to introduce the concept that there is no right without responsibility.

Resources

- teddy bear
- one pack per small group of the Rights and Responsibilities Jigsaw Pairs.

Starting Activity: For Classes and Small Groups

For this activity the children will need to be in a circle. Ask the children to stand up and for a volunteer to stand in the centre of the circle of children. Explain that the volunteer will be blindfolded and then a teddy bear will be placed somewhere in the circle. The task of the volunteer is to find the teddy bear. The other children in the circle are to use the following statements to help guide the volunteer:

- Cold means the volunteer is not near the teddy at all.
- Warm means they are getting nearer.
- Hot means they are very close.
- Very Hot means it is next to their foot and they have found the teddy.

You will need to set some ground rules for playing the game, for example, to say the help words softly and not shout them, to ensure that the child is safe in the circle and that if the volunteer is about to walk into someone they gently turn the person around guiding them back into the circle.

Main Activity: For Classes and Small Groups

Explain to the children that there is no right without a responsibility; give the example that if the right is to be treated kindly then you have the responsibility to treat others kindly. Ask the pupils if they can think of some more examples.

For large groups or classes you will need to ask pupils to form smaller groups of five to eight pupils. Provide each group with a set of Rights and Responsibilities Jigsaw Pairs (as group facilitator you will need to make sure that there is the exact number of card pieces as there are pupils, and that there are an even number of pupils per group). Explain to the pupils that they are to read their card (or ask someone to help them read it) and then walk around the room to find the pupil who has the other half of their jigsaw piece, that is, match each 'right' card with a 'responsibility' card. Jigsaw pieces need to fit together physically, that is, as jigsaw pieces as well as make sense in what they say. If necessary give the pupils some examples of which match and which do not match (these examples will need to be from the used jigsaw bits).

For Classes

Once everyone has completed their jigsaws each group is to read one of their statements out, for example, 'I have the right to be safe; my responsibility is to keep others safe.'

For Small Groups

Once everyone has found their pair and completed their jigsaws, ask them to sit back in the circle with their partner. Ask each pair in turn to read out their statements to the rest of the group, i.e. 'I have the right to be safe; my responsibility is to keep others safe.'

Ending Activity: For Classes and Small Groups

Each child in the class is to complete the following round:

- One way that I can keep other people safe is…

Rights and Responsibilities Jigsaw Pairs

Photocopy, or print from the CD-ROM, onto card and cut out individual pieces.

I have the Right to…

Be safe

My Responsibility is to…

Keep others safe

I have the Right to…

Say how I feel

My Responsibility is to…

Listen to others' feelings

I have the Right to…

Get help

My Responsibility is to…

Help others

I have the Right to...

My Responsibility is to...

Be cared for

Care for others

I have the Right to...

My Responsibility is to...

Learn

Not stop others learning

I have the Right to...

My Responsibility is to...

Choose

Let others choose

I have the Right to…

My Responsibility is to…

Join in

Not leave others out

I have the Right to…

My Responsibility is to…

Say no

Let others say no

I have the Right to…

My Responsibility is to…

Not be bullied

Not bully other people

Session Seven: Relationships

Aims

- to help individuals understand the importance of friends and friendship
- to enhance social skills around friendships
- to examine the skills involved in making friendship work.

Resources

- the My Friends worksheet – one per pupil
- one set of the Sentence Completion Cards.

Starting Activity: For Classes and Small Groups

Pass a Smile around the group, choose a pupil to start and ask them to pass a smile to the pupil on their left and continue this around the circle until the smile has been passed the entire way around the group and everyone has a smile on their face.

Main Activity: For Classes and Small Groups

Ask the group the following questions; you may want to record their answers onto the chalkboard or flip-chart:

- What is a friend?
- How do you know someone is your friend?
- What is being a friend about?
- What makes a good friend?

Provide each pupil with the worksheet titled My Friends and ask the pupils to complete it individually. Reconvene the group and ask for some feedback from the pupils about their answers to the questions on their sheet.

Ask the pupils the following questions:

- What do friends do for each other?
- How are friends the same as one another?
- How are friends different from one another?

Explain to the pupils that you have some sentences that they can finish about friends, that you will read the sentence and then ask for five or six volunteers to finish the sentence (if you are working with a small group all pupils can have a turn at finishing all sentences):

'Friendships can get broken because…'

'When I lose a friend I feel…'

'I would be a better friend if…'

Ending Activity: For Classes and Small Groups

Going around the circle/classroom firstly clockwise and then anti-clockwise ask the pupils to complete the following sentence positively:

'This is my friend… (name of the person on their left or right depending on direction you are going round) I like him\her because…'

(You may need to write this sentence on the chalkboard or flip-chart paper.)

My Friends

My friends are…

I like my friends because…

My friends like me because…

Sentence Completion Cards

Photocopy, or print from the CD-ROM, one set.

Friendships can get broken because…

When I lose a friend I feel…

I would be a better friend if…

Session Eight: Difference

Aims

- to explore the similarities and differences between pupils
- to help people celebrate each other's individual qualities.

Resources

- Similarities and Differences worksheet – one per pupil.

Starting Activity: For Classes and Small Groups

Each child is to introduce the person sitting on his or her left by saying their name, the colour of their hair and their eye colour, for example, 'This is Charlie she has blonde hair and blue eyes.'

Main Activity: For Classes and Small Groups

Ask pupils to change places with someone if they...

- have brown hair
- have green eyes
- have blue socks on
- are male
- like swimming
- are good at maths
- have been to a football match
- like pizza
- have a brother
- have a pet at home.

Each pupil is to talk to the pupil next to him or her to find out two things they have in common with each other. Allow time for pupils to give feedback using the following sentence:

'One thing we have in common is...'

'Another thing we have in common is...'

Provide pupils with the Similarities and Differences worksheet and explain that they are to walk around the room talking to different pupils in the group until they find a different pupil for each sentence on the sheet. When they find someone who matches the sentence they are to write the name next to the statement (if the writing ability is low you can just ask pupils to tick the box when they have found someone). For large groups pupils are not allowed to put the same person on their sheet twice and for small groups they are only allowed to use fellow group members twice (three times if the group is very low in numbers). When they have completed their sheet ask them to return to their chairs and sit down; they can still be asked questions by other pupils still filling in sheets.

If the reading and/or writing ability in the group is low it is worth going through each of the sentences verbally one at a time and simply asking pupils to pair with someone; for example, say to the pupils, 'Find someone in the group who has the same colour eyes as you and stand with them.' Once everyone has found someone move on to the next statement and so on until you have completed all statements.

Ending Activity: For Classes and Small Groups

Each child in the class is to complete the following round:

- We are all special. I am special because…

(You may need to write this sentence on the board or flip-chart.)

Similarities and Differences

How are we the same and how are we different?

Find someone in your class who...	Who is it?
Has the same colour eyes as you	
Has the same colour hair as you	
Likes watching TV	
Is the same age as you	
Likes singing	
Is a different height to you	
Likes chips	
Has a different name to you	
Has a different hobby to you	
Likes swimming	

Chapter Five

Emotional Health and Wellbeing Sessions for Key Stage 2 Pupils

Key Stage 2 Programme Delivery

The emotional health and wellbeing programme for Key Stage 2 comprises eight sessions; the sessions build on the content of that in Key Stage 1 and allow for the progression of skills. Each session lasts roughly thirty minutes and can be delivered to small groups or class groups. Where necessary, adaptations to activities for varying group sizes are provided. Additional sessions to evolve the programme, or extra activities to extend the sessions, can be delivered if the school wishes to add to the package provided. Good practice on preparing to deliver the programme is outlined at the start of Chapter Two and needs to be read by the facilitator prior to delivery.

The lesson plans take the facilitator step-by-step clearly through each session. The aims of each session are stated, lesson plans are provided and all the resources that are required are included at the end of each session (these can be photocopied or printed from the CD-ROM included with this book). The sessions are highly interactive and are based on visual, auditory and kinaesthetic (VAK) learning and apply a range of facilitation techniques.

The following is a brief account of the curriculum agenda:

Session One: This is Me

This session is about enabling pupils to express themselves and explore their identity in a safe way, to further explore what is unique about them and a gain a deeper awareness of their own 'self', celebrating their strengths and looking at ways to improve.

Session Two: Feelings

The focus of this session is around feelings. The session enables pupils to enhance their vocabulary, develop their ability in expressing a range of feelings and looks at how we respond to others people's feelings.

Session Three: Communication

This session continues to build on skills and goes on to examine different methods of communication. The session provides opportunities to develop group discussion, listening and feedback skills.

Session Four: Choice

Choice is about being aware of the options available and making a decision about them. This session allows pupils to practise making decisions, contribute to group decisions and understand the effects of their decisions.

Session Five: Personal Safety

Personal safety is the focus of this session. Pupils start to explore how they can remain safe when in physical and/or emotional difficulty. The concept of peer pressure is introduced and different ways of saying no assertively are practised.

Session Six: Keeping Others Safe

The theme of Session Six is about keeping others around you safe. The session aims to develop skills in communication, co-operation and working in groups, develop pupils recognition of when and how others may feel unsafe and explore ways that pupils can help one another be and stay safe, specifically in the context of bullying.

Session Seven: Relationships

The theme of this session is relationships. The session builds on pupils' skills of making and maintaining friendships and aims to help pupils recognise and understand other people's feelings when problems arise between friends.

Session Eight: Difference

Difference and diversity is the theme of this session. The session celebrates the difference and diversity of the class and pupils in the school and explores the ways that pupils are similar and different. The session provides opportunity to reflect on one's personal qualities and differences as well as help pupils recognise and challenge stereotypes and explore pupils' attitudes to difference.

Session One: This is Me

Aims

- to enable pupils to express themselves in a positive way

- to help pupils become more aware of what is unique about them

- to understand one's own strengths and areas for improvement.

Resources For Classes

- Getting Personal Jigsaw – one per pupil

- scissors

- card

- pens and pencils

- coloured crayons and pencils

- glue sticks.

Resources For Small Groups

- Getting Personal Tags – one set per pupil

- card

- pens and pencils

- coloured crayons and pencils

- string

- previously made wire mobile.

Starting Activity: For Classes and Small Groups

Ask each child in the class/group to complete the following round:

- I'm best known for being...

Main Activity: For Classes

Photocopy, or print from the CD-ROM, the Getting Personal Jigsaw onto card, ensuring you have enough for one per child.

Provide pupils with the Personal Jigsaw and ask them to cut it up into individual pieces. For each jigsaw piece the child is to record on the blank side a drawing, word or short sentence that reflects the instructions on the reverse of the jigsaw piece. Once they have completed all topics ask them to remake their jigsaw and then Sellotape it back together again, with their pictures and words facing one way and the descriptors facing the other.

The pictures can be used for a display in the classroom to remind the pupils of their positive qualities and their strengths. Instructions on the jigsaw are:

- draw or write what you are most proud of
- draw or write a special skill you have
- draw or write something that you do for fun
- draw or write your favourite food
- draw or write something you are really interested in
- draw or write about you and your family
- draw or write about something you are good at
- draw or write the thing you are known best for
- draw or write something you dream of.

Main Activity: For Small Groups

Photocopy the Getting Personal Tags onto card, ensuring you have enough for one set per child.

Ask each pupil to record on the blank side of the tag a drawing, word or short sentence that reflects the instructions on the reverse of the tag. Once they have completed all the tags they are to reconvene in a group. Ask pupils to put their tags in the following order:

- something you are most proud of
- a special skill you have
- something that you do for fun
- your favourite food
- something you are really interested in
- you and your family
- something you are good at
- the thing you are known best for
- something you dream of.

Using a mobile pre-made out of wire hangers ask each child in turn to complete the first sentence; as they complete it ask them to come and attach the tag to the mobile using a piece of string. Work through each of the tags in turn until all are hung on the mobile.

The mobile can be used for a display in the classroom to remind the pupils of their positive qualities and their strengths.

Ending Activity: For Classes

Ask each child in the class to complete the following round while showing their classmates their picture:

- This is what I like and I am good at. One thing I would like to get better at is…

Ending Activity: For Groups

Ask each child to turn to the person on their left and say, 'You have lots of strengths and good qualities', and then turn to the person on the right and say, 'I have lots of strengths and good qualities.'

Getting Personal Jigsaw

Cut your jigsaw into individual pieces being careful to cut along the lines. Now draw or write on the blank side following the instruction. When you have done all the statements remake your jigsaw with your words and pictures face up; you will need to fit the pieces together to make the jigsaw.

Draw or write what you are most proud of on the other side of this jigsaw piece.

Draw or write a special skill you have on the other side of this jigsaw piece.

Draw or write something that you do for fun on the other side of this jigsaw piece.

Draw or write your favourite food on the other side of this jigsaw piece.

Draw or write something you are really interested in on the other side of this jigsaw piece.

Draw or write about you and your family on the other side of this jigsaw piece.

Draw or write about something you are good at on the other side of this jigsaw piece.

Draw or write the thing you are known best for on the other side of this jigsaw piece.

Draw or write something you dream of on the other side of this jigsaw piece.

Getting Personal Tags

Draw or write what you are most proud of on the other side of this tag.

Draw or write a special skill you have on the other side of this tag.

Draw or write something that you do for fun on the other side of this tag.

Draw or write your favourite food on the other side of this tag.

Draw or write something you are really interested in on the other side of this tag.

Draw or write about you and your family on the other side of this tag.

Draw or write about something you are good at on the other side of this tag.

Draw or write the thing you are known best for on the other side of this tag.

Draw or write something you dream of on the other side of this tag.

Session Two: Feelings

Aims

- to enable pupils to express a range of different feelings
- to develop a feelings vocabulary
- to develop appropriate responses to others feelings.

Resources For Classes

- white A4 card - one piece per pupil
- pencils and pens
- coloured crayons and pencils
- blu-tac.

Resources For Small Groups

- white A4 card – one sheet between three
- pencils and pens
- coloured crayons and pencils
- Feelings Sentence Completion Tag Lines.

Starting Activity: For Classes and Small Groups

Choose one pupil to start and ask them to say a feeling that begins with the letter A, move to the next person who is to state a feeling beginning with the letter B, continue to move around the pupils working your way through the alphabet stating feelings corresponding to each letter.

Main Activity: For Classes

Provide pupils with a piece of white A4 card, pencils and coloured crayons. Pupils are to be given a letter of the alphabet and their task is to think of a feeling beginning with that letter and design a poster that represents that feeling. The completed poster can be used to create a frieze frame around the classroom.

Main Activity: For Small Groups

As a group generate a list of feelings, for example, happy, sad, angry, shy, proud, nervous, and excited. Ask the pupils to form small groups of three and provide each with a piece of paper and a feelings word from the list generated. Each group's task is to make a poster by adding other associated feelings in relation to the original feeling word they have been given. For example if the feeling word is 'happy' other associated feelings may be joyful, smiley, excited, merry, jolly, pleased, delighted and so on; explain to the pupils that there are no right or wrong answers and to come up with as many ideas as possible and to add drawings if they wish. Ask pupils to keep their work as neat as possible as they will be used for posters.

Reconvene the group and ask each small group to feed back their ideas in turn. After each group has responded ask others if they can think of other ideas to add to the posters.

Ending Activity: For Classes

In turn each child in the class is to hold their poster up, say what letter of the alphabet it is, what the feeling is and something they could do if people felt this way. For example:

My poster is S for Sad, if someone was sad I could…

Ending Activity: For Groups

Place the Feelings Sentence Completion Tag Lines face down in the centre of the circle; ask each pupil in turn to pick one up, read it out and complete it. Continue until each person in the group has completed a tag line. Tag lines are:

- When someone calls me a name I feel…
- When someone shares their toys with me I feel…
- When my teacher says well done I feel…
- When I fall out with my friends I feel…
- When I have a new present I feel…
- When I argue with someone I feel…
- When I play alone I feel…
- When someone says something nice to me a feel…
- When I fall over and hurt myself I feel…
- When someone pushes in the dinner queue I feel…

Feelings Sentence Completion Tag Lines

When someone calls me a name I feel...

When someone shares their toys with me I feel...

When my teacher says well done I feel...

When I fall out with my friends I feel...

When I have a new present I feel...

When I argue with someone I feel...

When I play alone I feel...

When someone says something nice to me I feel...

When I fall over and hurt myself I feel...

When someone pushes in the dinner queue I feel...

Session Three: Communication

Aims

- to explore the different methods of communication
- to provide opportunity to develop group discussion skills
- to practise listening and feedback skills.

Resources

- flip-chart paper
- flip-chart pens.

Starting Activity: For Classes and Small Groups

Play a game of Chinese Whispers: explain to the pupils that one person will start and think of a short sentence. The first pupil will whisper the sentence to the next pupil, who will then whisper it to the person next to them. The sentence continues to be whispered from one pupil to the next until all in the group have had a turn. The last pupil is to state the sentence that they heard. The task is to pass the sentence around all pupils without the words changing but it's not as easy as you might think!

Main Activity: For Classes and Small Groups

Ask the pupils to get into a line based on when their birthday is, with January at one end and December at the other. However, the pupils are not allowed to talk to each other to do this.

Go along the line of pupils and ask them which month their birthday is, to check if everyone managed to get into the right place. Going along the line starting at one end split the group into smaller groups of four or five. Provide each group with a piece of flip-chart paper and some flip-chart pens; ask them to record words, short sentences or pictures of the different methods there are to communicate with people. For example, by text, talking, writing, sign language and so on. Allow five minutes before reconvening the group. Each group is to take their turn in feeding back. The facilitator is to record all the methods of communication onto one flipchart or the blackboard.

Ask the pupils to form a pair with someone that they do not know very well. In the pairs label one pupil A and the other B. A is to listen to B while they talk about the best present that they ever received, what it was and why they liked it. Once they have done this roles are reversed, that is, B now listens to A while they talk about the best present they have received. Then ask the pupils to join with another pair. Explain that the task now is for A's to feed back about what B's said about their present and then B's to feed back about what A's said. As the facilitator you may need to have a timing signal (clap hands, ring a bell) to indicate it is time to change over.

Ending Activity: For Classes and Small Groups

Each child in the class is to complete the following round:

- I know my partner listened to me because…

Session Four: Choices

Aims

- to give pupils the opportunity to contribute to decisions
- to help pupils understand how their decision affects others
- to help pupils recognise their ability to make choices.

Resources

- list of the class rules
- prepared flip-chart.

Starting Activity: For Classes and Small Groups

Ask each child in the class to complete the following round:

- One choice I have made today is…

Main Activity: For Classes and Small Groups

Remind the children of the school or classroom rules and explain that today's session will be spent looking more closely at these rules.

If the pupils are not already working in groups or on tables, split the class in to about five small groups and provide each group with one of the school or class rules. If this activity is being done with one small group ask pupils to work in pairs or threes or alternatively work together as one large group.

In their groups/pairs ask pupils to think about and record their ideas with reference to their specific rule on the following:

- the effects on teacher, pupils and classes when people follow the rules
- the effects on the teacher, pupil and classes when people do not follow the rules.

Provide each group with a piece of flip-chart paper that on one side has the three headings: effects on teacher, effects on pupil, effects on class and titled When Rules are Followed and on the other side has the same three headings but titled When Rules are Not Followed.

For example:

Side One:

When Rules are Followed		
Effects on teacher	Effects on pupil	Effects on class

Side Two:

When Rules are Not Followed		
Effects on teacher	Effects on pupil	Effects on class

When the groups have exhausted their ideas, ask each group in turn to feed back some of their ideas.

Make a summary statement about the negative effects and consequences of making decisions that go against rules. You may also want to relate this to choices in other areas of life where people have made the wrong choice and draw on the effects that this has had (for example, footballers fouling, breaking the law, athletes taking performance enhancing drugs). This may prompt a discussion with the pupils.

Ending Activity: For Classes and Small Groups

Ask each child in the class to complete the following round:

- Another rule I know about outside school is… This is important because…

An example that you could provide for the children is, 'Another rule I know about outside school is to stop, look and listen at a busy road. This is important because it keeps me safe.'

Session Five: Personal Safety

Aims

- to explore how we can stay safe when we may be in 'emotional' or 'physical' difficulty
- to introduce the concept of peer pressure
- to examine different way of saying NO.

Resources

- flip-chart paper and pens
- What is Expected of You? worksheet – one per pupil.

Starting Activity: For Classes and Small Groups

Provide each pupil with the worksheet What is Expected of You? and ask them to record the things that other people expect them to do to keep themselves safe.

Ask each pupil in turn to feed back one idea.

Main Activity: For Classes and Small Groups

Write the following sentence on the chalkboard.

How can we stay safe even if…

- we get left out on the playground
- we have a busy road to cross on the way to school
- we are scared about our SATs
- we feel upset at school
- we have fallen out with our friends
- we are teased
- we lose our dinner money.

(These are suggestions and you may wish to come up with some ideas of your own that are more relevant to the class.)

Split the class into six groups, or if you are working with a small group split them into pairs, using the following game:

Ask pupils to line up in alphabetical order without speaking. Once they have done it test it out by asking everyone to say their name out loud in turn starting at A (the start of the line hopefully). If you are pairing the pupils pair them with the person next to them, for a small group break the line into equal sized groups.

Once in their groups or pairs provide each group or pair with one of the 'How can we stay safe even if…' sentences, a flip-chart and flip-chart pens. Ask the group to come up with at least ten ways in which we can stay safe if this was to happen.

Reconvene the group and ask each group to feed back in turn.

Ending Activity: For Classes and Small Groups

Explain to the pupil's that sometimes we do things because our friends do and we are too scared, worried or afraid to say, 'No' in case our friends think badly of us. Explain that this is sometimes called peer pressure. Ask pupils if they can think of characters on the TV who have done things just because their friends have. Discuss what the person might be feeling as a result of doing this, why they might have done this and what the effects were of their decision.

Explain to the pupils that sometimes we have to be firm and say, 'NO' if we don't want to do things that spark feelings of being unsafe.

Ask each child in the class to complete the following round:

- When I don't want to do something I could say…

(For example, thanks but no thanks; do you want to do XXX instead; I don't think that is a good idea I'll pass thanks; that is a bit scary I don't want to be involved, are you sure you do?)

What is Expected of You?

What do my mum and dad expect me to do to keep myself safe?

(For example, come home at the time I say I will come home, tell them if something is upsetting me.)

What do my teachers expect me to do to keep myself safe?

(For example, follow the school rules, tell them if the work is to hard or easy.)

What do my friends expect me to do to keep myself safe?

(For example, to stay together if we are out, to play nicely with them.)

What to I expect myself to do to keep myself safe?

(For example, tell someone if I am worried, follow the school rules.)

Session Six: Keeping Others Safe

Aims

- to develop skills in communication, co-operation and working in groups

- to develop pupils' recognition of when and how others may feel unsafe

- to explore ways that pupils can help one another be and stay safe, specifically in the context of bullying.

Resources

- teddy bear

- Problem-solving worksheet – one per small group.

Starting Activity: For Classes and Small Groups

Explain to the children that a volunteer will be chosen to find a teddy that is in a hidden location in the room, the place of the teddy will be unknown to the volunteer but all other members of the group will know the location. The difficulty for the volunteer will be that they will be blindfolded and the other children in the class have to guide the child to the teddy bear, using forward, backward, left and right directions.

Main Activity: For Classes and Small Groups

Provide each table with a problem-solving worksheet. If you are working with a small group work together as one group or if there are two facilitators split the group in two. Explain that their task is to work as a group and complete the sheet to explore feeling safe and what they can do to help.

Allow 20 minutes to work on this.

Reconvene the group and take feedback from each table.

Ending Activity: For Classes and Small Groups

Ask each child in the class to complete the following round:

- One way I keep others safe is…

Problem-solving

You have got a new pupil in your class.

What is their name? _____ How old are they?_____

The pupil is new to the area and new to the school, what things may they be worried about? (Come up with as many ideas as possible.)

_____

_____

_____

_____

How do you think they feel being the 'new' person in school?

_____

_____

_____

_____

What can we do to help? (Come up with as many ways that you can think of.)

_____

_____

_____

_____

_____

_____

_____

Session Seven: Relationships

Aims

- to explore the skills involved in making and maintaining friends
- to recognise other people's feelings when there are problems with friendships
- to think about the skills that pupils possess in relation to friendships.

Resources

- pen
- storyboard.

Starting Activity: For Classes and Small Groups

As a group think of all the things (qualities, skills, attributes and other ideas) that make up a friend:

- someone who lives near you
- someone who shares
- someone who knows you well
- someone who won't make judgements
- someone who listens
- someone who plays with you
- someone who is kind and caring
- someone who is good to spend time with
- someone who keeps secrets.

As the pupils come up with these record them onto the board or flip-chart.

Ask pupils to look at the list and explain that some of the things on the list are skills that we possess in order to make friendships work (that is, being non judgemental, being a good listener, being kind and caring). Ask for one volunteer at a time from the group to come up and circle one of the items on the board or flip-chart that is a skill and say why it is important in friendships, continue until all the skills have been circled and discussed.

Main Activity: For Classes and Small Groups

Work with the pupils as a whole group working through the storyboard provided.

Ending Activity: For Classes and Small Groups

Ask the pupils to stand up and sit down if...

- your friends are important to you
- you have friends in other classes.

Ask the pupils to stand up, turn around and sit down if...

- you have friends in other schools
- you have a best friend.

Ask the pupils to stand up, turn around, jump in the air and sit down if...

- you have never fallen out with your friends
- you make up quickly with your friends after an argument.

Storyboard

> Ben and Adam (or Sally and Beena) are best friends at school; they have known each other for a long time. Ben and Adam always play together at play and lunch-time, they tell each other their secrets and enjoy spending time together after school and in the holidays. Ben and Adam have fallen out. What reasons might Ben and Adam have fallen out for?

As a class, list all the possible reasons why Ben and Adam may have fallen out and record all the possible reasons on to the board or flip-chart.

Choose one of the reasons that the pupils have come up with for Ben and Adam falling out (circle the one you have chosen) and then ask the pupils firstly how Adam feels (think about and record all the possible feelings on the right hand side of the board) and then how Ben feels (think about and record all the possible feeling on the left hand side of the board). If there is a third party involved create three columns and also record the possible ways that they could be feeling.

Now ask the class or group what Ben and Adam could do to make up and become friends again and record all their ideas on the board/flip-chart.

This activity helps pupils recognise why people fall out, the feelings of others involved when there are problems in friendships and what to do to help make things better. As the facilitator it is worth recapping on the whole story that the class or group have created and elaborate the learning at each stage and the skills involved with friendships.

Storyboard Example

Ben and Adam (or Sally and Beena) are best friends at school; they have known each other for a long time. Ben and Adam always play together at play and lunch-time, they tell each other their secrets and enjoy spending time together after school and in the holidays. Ben and Adam have fallen out.

What reasons might Ben and Adam have fallen out for?

- Adam would not share his sweets.
- Ben told John one of Adams secrets.
- One of them did a dirty tackle on the other in football.
- One of them ignored the other.
- They choose to play with different friends.
- Someone said that Adam said Ben was silly.
- Ben called Adam a name.

Imagine that Ben told John one of Adam's secrets, how might:

A. Ben feel	B. Adam feel	C. John feel
• Guilty	• Hatred	• Confused
• Upset	• Anger	• Guilty
• Worried	• Sad	• Blamed
• Frightened	• Embarrassed	• Worried
• Jealous	• Worried	• Carefree

What can Ben and Adam do to make up and become friends again?

- Talk about it.
- Express how they feel and say what they want to happen.
- Ask a third party to help them.
- Discuss the importance of secrets.

Session Eight: Difference

Aims

- to celebrate difference and diversity
- to explore the ways that the group or class are similar and different.
- to provide opportunity to reflect on one's personal qualities and differences
- to help pupils recognise and challenge stereotypes
- to explore pupils' attitudes to difference.

Resources

- Human Bingo sheets – one per pupil
- VIP worksheet – one per pupil
- Sentence Completion Cards – one set.

Starting Activity: For Classes and Small Groups

Provide each pupil with a Human Bingo Sheet and explain that they are to wander around the room and find someone who fits each of the statements; they are not allowed to use anyone more than once (if in small groups then they should not use the same person more than twice) and when they have finished their sheet shout BINGO.

Main Activity: For Classes and Small Groups

Pupils will need to sit in a circle for this activity. Ask for a volunteer to stand in the centre of the circle and then move their chair away.

Ask the person in the centre to think of something that they have done, enjoy doing, a place they have been or a hobby that they have that they think no one else in the room has done, they are to say this out loud.

If someone else in the room has also done this, ask them to swap places with the person in the centre and state something they have done that they feel they do not share with anyone else in the room.

If with the first volunteer no one has done this, ask them to state something they think they have in common with everyone in the room, this maybe something as simple as, 'I brushed my teeth this morning.' Anyone who has this is common with the volunteer changes places.

Whilst people are changing places the volunteer needs to find an empty chair to sit on. The person left standing is now to follow this process, that is, firstly state one thing they feel they do not have in common with anyone and then one thing they feel they have in common with everyone. Continue until everyone has had a go or the group is mixed.

As a group recall some of the things that they had in common and some of the things that were different about people in the room.

Ask pupils to complete the following sentences in turn (with larger groups you may wish to read the sentence and ask for a handful of volunteers to complete it. Use the sentence completion cards as this will help remind pupils of the wording.

- If we were all the same it would be...

- Being different is good because...

- One stereotype that people have is... (You may need to explain the concept of a stereotype to pupils.)

- If someone was picked on for being different I would...

Provide each pupil with the VIP worksheet. Ask the pupils if anyone knows what the acronym VIP stands for. Explain that while the acronym is well known for standing for Very Important Person we can also think of it to mean Very Individual Person. Explain that all of us are important and all of us are individual. Ask pupils to individually complete the VIP worksheet.

Reconvene the group and ask the pupils to feed back in turn one of the sentences from their VIP sheet.

Ending Activity: For Classes and Small Groups

Ask each child in the class to complete the following rounds:

- One way I am the same as other people is...

- One way I am different of other people is...

Human Bingo

Someone who has a birthday in the summer months is _____	Someone who has a pet at home is _____	Someone who has a hobby that involves being outdoors is _____
Someone who collects something is _____	Someone who has a brother and a sister is _____	Someone who likes to go to the cinema is _____
Someone who is a good listener is _____	Someone who has visited the zoo is _____	Someone who likes to drink milk is _____

Sentence Completion Cards

Photocopy, or print from the CD-ROM, one set.

If we were all the same it would be

Being different is good because

One stereotype that people have is

If someone was picked on for being different I would

VIP   VIP   VIP   VIP

Very **Important** Person
Very **Individual** Person

I like myself because:

The best thing about being me is:

I have the power to:

I am really good at:

People admire me for:

I feel important when:

My friends like me because:

People praise me for:

I am proud that I:

Bibliography and Resources

Bliss, T. & Tetley, J. (1993) *Circle Time a Resource Book for Infant, Junior and Secondary Schools* Bristol: Lucky Duck Publishing.

Borba, M. (1989) *Esteem Builders*. California: Jalmar Press.

Britton, F. (2000) *Discovering Citizenship Through Active Learning in the Community*. London: CSV Education for Citizenship.

Burt, S., Davis, G., Lister, J., Morgan, R. & O'Shea, S. (1999) *Six Years of Circle Time*. Bristol: Lucky Duck Publishing.

Centre for Citizenship Studies in Education www.le.ac.uk/education/centres/citizenship

Darton, K. (1998) Children and Young People and Mental Health Fact Sheet: Updated by Stewart, G. (2001)

Citizenship Foundation (2001) *Citizenship Education: What's it got to do with me?*

Cole, J.D. & Dodge, K.A. (1988) Multiple Scores of data on Social Behaviour and Social Status in The School: A Cross Age Comparison. *Child Development*. 59, 815-829.

Coppersmith, S. (1967) *The Antecedents of Self-Esteem*. San Francisco: WH Freeman.

Cowie, H. & Pecherek, A. (1994) *Counselling: Approaches and Issues in Education*. London: David Fulton.

Curry, M. & Bromfield, C. (1998) *Circle Time In-Service Training Manual*. Staffordshire: NASEN

Danson, H., France-Jaswowska, A., Jefferies, B., & Weisselberg, A. (1997) *The Samaritans Youth Pack - Helping You Help Young People*. Slough: Samaritans.

Department for Education and Skills www.dfes.gov.uk

Department of Health (2003) Using the National Healthy Schools Standard to Raise Boys Achievement. Yorkshire: DoH.

DfEE (1999a) National Healthy Schools Standard – Getting Started: A Guide for Schools. Nottingham: DfEE.

DfEE (1999b) National Healthy Schools Standard Guidance. Nottingham: DfEE.

DfES (2002) What is Citizenship? www.DfES.gov.uk/Citizenship.

DfES & DoH (2003) National Healthy Schools Standard – Confirming Healthy Schools Achievement. www.wiredforhealth.gov.uk

Duck, S.W. (1991) *Friends For Life*. Hemel Hempstead: Harvester-Wheatsheaf.

Faulkner, D. & Miell, D. (1993) Settling Into School: The Importance of Early Friendships For The Development Of Children's Social Understanding and Communicative Competence. *International Journal of Early Years Education*, 1, 1, 23-45.

Greenfield, S. (2000) in Hunt, C. (1999) *Family Links - The Nurturing Programme*. Oxford: Family Links.

Gorden, S. & Litt, S. (1989) *Try Again Red Riding Hood - A New Look at An Old Story*. Australia: Essence Publications.

Korfkamp, T. (1998) *Raising Self-Esteem and Building Self-Confidence Through Group Work*. Wolverhampton: WISARD.

Kurtz, Z. 1992. *With Health in Mind - Mental Health Care for children and Young People*. Action for Sick Children with South West Thames Regional Health Authority.

Lees, J. & Plant, S. (2000) *PASSPORT ~ A framework for Personal and Social Development*. London: Calouste Gulbenkian Foundation.

Lemington Spa LEA (1999) Warwickshire Health Promoting School. (WHPSS) *Quality Standards for Healthy Eating*. Leamington Spa: EDS Publications.

Long, R. (1999) Learning to Wave: Some Everyday Guidelines for Stress Management. Staffs: NASEN.

Margetts,D., Nault, S., Selk-Yerges, L. and Smaglik, L (1996) Feeling Safe and Standing Strong. US: ASTOP INC.

Maslow, A. (1954) Maslow's Hierarchy of Needs in Gross, R.D. (1987) *Psychology: The Science of Mind and Behaviour*. London: Hodder & Stoughton.

Maslow, A. (1970) in Gross, R.D (1987) *Psychology: The Science of Mind and Behaviour*. London: Hodder & Stoughton.

Mind (National Asoociation for Mental Health) 15-19 Broadway, London E15 4BQ www.mid.org.uk

NHS (2002) *Making Best Use of The National Healthy Schools Standard - A Guide for PCTs*. London: DfES.

Nottingham LEA (1999) *National Healthy School Standard Getting Started ~ A Guide for Schools*. Nottingham: DFEE Publications.

Office for National Statistic, Population and Selected Statistics (1999) www.mind.org.uk

Parker, J.G & Asher, S.R. (1987) Peer Relations And Later Peer Adjustment: Are Low Accepted Children At Risk? *Psychological Bulletin*, 102, 357-389.

Persona Dolls Training, 51 Granville Road, London N12 0JH www.persona-doll-training.org

Roger, C. (1961) in Danson, H., France-Jaswowska, A., Jefferies, B., & Weisselberg, A. (1997) The Samaritans Youth Pack - Helping You Help Young People. Slough: Samaritans.

School Councils UK www.schoolcouncils.org

Shrewsbury LEA (2002) Schools For Health ~ Guidance for the Healthy Eating Theme. Shrewsbury: Publications and Designs Unit.

Smith, A. et al (2000) The Scale of Occupational Stress: A Further Analysis of The Impact of Demographic Factors & Type of Job in Warwickshire Education Authority (2002) Quality Standards for Emotional Health & Wellbeing (Including Bullying) Warwickshire.

Steel, L. (2000) *Listening for a Change: The Development of the Self-Concept*. Horsham: YSP.

Steel, L. (2000) *Listening for a Change: Using Emotional Intelligence to Manage Anger*. Horsham: YSP.

TES (2003) Times Article, 1st August 2003 p2:TES.

The Association for Citizenship Teaching (ACT) www.teachingcitizenship.org.uk

The Child Psychotherapy Trust, Fact Sheet One: Won't They Just Grow Out Of It? www.ming.org.uk

The Citizenship Foundation www.citfou.org.uk

The Institute for Citizenship www.citizen.org.uk

The Stress Consultancy www.stressmanagementtraining.biz.com

Stress Management Session One: A Distance Learning Training Course. Sheffield: Pinders Ltd.

Warwick, I. & Douglas, N. (1999) *Safe For All: A best practice guide to prevent homophobic bullying in secondary schools*. London: Citizenship 21.

White, T., Chillery, M., Colley, K., Down, J., Hamilton, J., Lamb, V., Oliver, I., Rathbone, J. & Sayer, A. (2002) Warwickshire LEA - Quality Standards for Emotional Health and Wellbeing (Including Bullying). Warwickshire: LEA.

White, M. (1999) *Magic Circles: Building self-Esteem Through Circle Time* Bristol. Lucky Duck Publishing.

www.bbc.co.uk/health/emotional

www.dfes.gov.uk/mentalhealth

www.mind.org.uk

www.wiredforhealth.gov.uk